P9-DXS-432

CONDUCTING

EMIL KAHN

CONDUCTING

THE FREE PRESS, NEW YORK

Collier-Macmillan Limited, London

A DIVISION OF THE MACMILLAN COMPANY

Printed in the United States of America

Collier-Macmillan Canada, Ltd., Toronto, Ontario

printing number
4 5 6 7 8 9 10

LIBRARY OF CONGRESS CATALOG CARD NUMBER: 65-21137

Acknowledgments

THE GREATEST INCENTIVE to write this book came from the musicians of the various great orchestras he has had the opportunity to conduct, and from the students of his college orchestra, opera workshop, and those that attended his conducting classes at Montclair State College. The author thanks Dr. Arthur Christmann, Professor of Music at Montclair State College and instructor at the Juilliard School of Music, New York City, for his professional assistance. He is, furthermore, thankful to members of his family for the help he received from them in organizing the book.

The author wishes to thank the firm of G. Schirmer, Inc., New York City, for permission to use excerpts from Gluck's *Don Juan* Overture (copyright 1951), Dittersdorf's *Tournament of Temperaments* (copyright 1956), Handel's *Watermusic* (copyright 1958), and Gluck's *At the Court of Maria Theresa,* (copyright 1960), arranged by him. The author also wishes to thank the firm of Boosey & Hawkes for permission to use a passage from Bartok's *Concerto For Orchestra* (copyright 1946 by Hawkes & Son [London] Ltd. Reprinted by permission of Boosey & Hawkes Inc.); as well as the original Universal Edition, Vienna, for permission to include an excerpt from Mahler's Ninth Symphony (copyright 1912).

Contents

PART FOUR

INTERPRETATION 127

PART FIVE

PRACTICAL MATTERS 167

PART SIX

ADDITIONAL CONDUCTING SKILLS 183

Introduction

TO BECOME the leader of a great orchestra is the dream of many a young musician. One of the major obstacles to learning his craft, however, is the fact that the student has little chance to practice on his instrument, the orchestra. Usually he can consider himself lucky if during his college or conservatory conducting course he has a chance to lead an orchestra for more than a few minutes a week. Compared to the many hours a day instrumentalists practice, in order to master their instruments, this is only a trifle.

The student conductor must become acquainted first of all with all the *elements* of his craft, which cover such a wide area that they can easily fill an entire conducting course. The intricate beat-patterns needed for complicated rhythmical designs, for example, will only confuse him if he has no chance to try them with a competent orchestra. He can only acquire the skill to conduct such patterns when he becomes experienced in leading orchestras; for this reason the student of conducting should have more opportunities for actual practice.

This book gives the student directions for practicing conducting from the very first day; in each lesson he will learn if his beat is adequate to any particular problem. Therefore, conducting while listening to a recording is not recommended. The student will not conduct the recording but will be led by it. He will not discover if his beat is effective. On the other hand, recordings may be useful when studying a new or unfamiliar work: they can be a short-cut, allowing one to become acquainted with the actual sound of a piece and with a master interpretation. It is advisable, however, for a serious student of the art of conducting to study a score thoroughly *without* this help. Thereafter a comparison with a recording may be of additional aid.

The beat is only one of the many elements a conductor has to master. Ear training, score reading, knowledge of all the instruments and their technique, as well as matters of tempo, dynamics, and style, are additional fields of study and practice.

One of the most important faculties, that of being able to inspire an orchestra, cannot be taught. Mere "personality," however, without sufficient training and knowledge can breed charlatanism.

The student should concentrate on the fundamentals of conducting. By far the largest number of new conductors will be required for the important job of training school orchestras, since competent elementary and high school conductors have never been needed as urgently as they are today. Since the last war the number of school orchestras has decreased alarmingly. The interest in good music has definitely grown – partly because one can now hear it almost "live" on high-fidelity and stereophonic records – but youngsters have lost interest in playing stringed instruments. They have discovered they can achieve a minimum of proficiency on clarinet or trumpet much faster than on violin or cello, thereby becoming eligible to enter the attractively clad marching band. Later they may even attain jobs in well-paying dance orchestras.

There is nothing wrong with this, especially since the quality of school bands has been improving. Still, if there are no school orchestras, many of our musically inclined young people will have no chance to play the works of the masters in the original. What is even more disconcerting, our professional orchestras – and American orchestras are among the finest in the world – will gradually be deprived of the necessary string players.

Any professional starts studying his instrument while still in school. An incentive for this study must come from the school itself. The best way to arouse interest in playing stringed instruments is to have a good school orchestra – and the quality of the orchestra will depend mainly on the ability of the conductor. A qualified and inspiring leader can develop a group into the pride of an institution.* It is the main purpose of this book to help train such conductors. The material is selected in order to give

* Fortunately, music educators have become aware of the danger threatened by the decrease of string playing. Some elementary and high schools are doing an excellent job with special string programs, generally taught by string experts. This book should be a welcome help in perfecting their capacity as orchestra leaders. Let us repeat that talent and inspiration alone cannot make good conductors. They will also need the tools for their profession.

the most comprehensive background for building an instrumental group.

Although this book is written with the emphasis on non-professional orchestral conducting, the basic rules apply equally to professional orchestras, as well as to bands and choruses. Special chapters have been included to show some of the problems of conducting these groups. A chapter on opera conducting has also been included which should be welcomed by the increasing number of young conductors — high school, college, and professional — interested in that field.

This textbook is written with the classroom in mind. It may well be used for self-teaching, however, preferably with the assistance of a singer or instrumentalist. Young conductors already leading orchestras should welcome it for the additional guidance it gives them, and should find the *Workbook* especially valuable.

HOW TO USE THIS BOOK

If this textbook is being used in class, suggestions for its study depend on whether it is to be used for a one-semester, two-semester, or two-year course. Conducting embraces such a large field of knowledge and practice that a one-semester course can only scratch the surface — unless score reading, advanced ear training, style, and thorough knowledge of the instruments have been dealt with in previous courses. The purpose of this book will best be fulfilled when instruction is scheduled for two years. By carefully organizing the material, however, an instructor may be able to fit it into one.

Parts One and Two, dealing with different skills, may be used simultaneously for the first classes. Each class should be divided into three sections: Ear Training, Score Reading, Beat, with the major portion reserved for Beat. These skills should be developed throughout the course. The teacher will omit one or the other in some class periods, should he feel his students need an introduction to other chapters of the book. The "knowledge" part (Three and Four), Practical Matters (Five), and Additional Conducting

Skills (Six) should be taken up as soon as the students have grasped the basic contents of Parts One and Two.

The chapter on repertory suggestions has been included mainly for reference purposes, but it may be valuable for discussion in class.

Major problems are usually accompanied by examples from music literature or — when deemed necessary — by special exercises made up for the purpose. Examples should be studied by the students. The more acquaintance an aspiring conductor gains with standard literature the better. The scores should be easily accessible in libraries. On the other hand, students should be encouraged to build their own libraries of the masterworks.

The Beat

ONE

WHEN we first learn to write we are taught to adhere very closely to the letter-patterns of the alphabet. Later, as we develop individual and fluent handwriting, our script may stray far from the original forms we have been taught. It is much the same when it comes to the established beat-patterns of conducting. If a student tries to imitate great conductors who have acquired very individual beats (to which their own orchestras have gradually become accustomed) he may well be unintelligible to inexperienced players. Individuality will develop without special effort when the conductor has talent and is not a mere time-beater.

1 *Beating different meters*

2/4 METER

Beat-patterns are the fundamentals of conducting, and must become second nature to the student. To begin with, the diagram of the 2/4 meter is simple as in Fig. 1.

Fig. 1

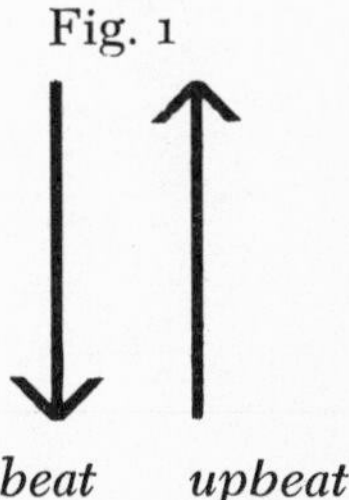

In actual conducting, the motion of the right arm should be elastic on both beats. The downbeat springs back, slightly to the right, then stops (except in legato passages, in which the flow of the beat should never be interrupted). On the upbeat the hand does not move straight upward; first it moves a short distance downward, toward the left—making a figure resembling a small hook— before returning to the starting point.

The actual beat-patterns are shown in Figs. 2, 3, and 4.

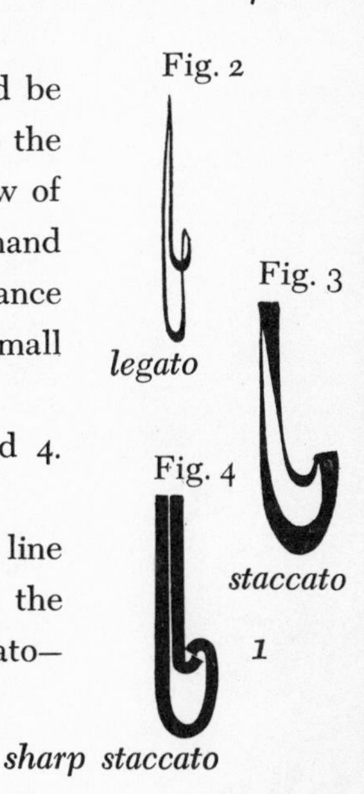

The stress is where the line becomes heaviest. When the line thins out, the motion slows down. In a sharp staccato beat, the stress is carried through each beat. For conducting non-legato—

and portato—passages, the legato pattern should be used, with a very slight stop at the end of each beat (intermediate beat).

The 2/4 beat should be practiced while the instructor plays any 2/4 meter music on the piano (slow, fast, legato, intermediate, and staccato).* The student should start when he has gained a "feeling" for the meter and character of the music. The right arm should hang comfortably; the elbow should be held neither too close to the body nor lifted too high. The left hand should not be used for these exercises: students too easily get into the habit of waving both hands instead of using the left for special purposes.

CHARACTER OF BEAT

The size of the beat-pattern depends largely upon the character and tempo of the music. A light, rather fast staccato does not require more than small, sharp motions of the wrist.† For a more vigorous beat the forearm should be used. With growing experience the student will discover that a large beat, involving the whole arm, is seldom necessary even for dramatic passages. In slow, sustained music the beats should never halt, but the stress of each beat should always be clear. This slowing up must occur toward the end of each motion; otherwise, even in an adagio, the beat becomes "spineless." From the beginning the student should get used to these elementary modifications in

* In the Introduction, students were discouraged from using recordings. In these preliminary exercises, however, where the student does not actually conduct but should get a feel for the beat, recordings may help. A selection may be made from the many examples in Chapter Two. Pieces especially suited for the purpose are marked #. The tempo and character, suggested in each of these examples, should help to determine what kind of beat is needed. Since the starting beat is discussed in the next chapter — and since it is practically impossible to start beating exactly with the start on a recording — a few measures of the recording should precede the student's beat. During these exercises the student should conduct from a score; for the beginning a piano reduction is permissible.

† There is a school of conducting that rejects the use of the wrist and advises the use of forearm and hand in a straight line (relaxed and not stiff), contending that the beat will be steadier and therefore clearer. A decision about which way is better depends on the student's individuality and — while this author has achieved best results with using the wrist — a number of highly accomplished conductors avoid it.

conducting different tempos, different dynamics, and different styles. If the music has an especially sustained character (tenuto) the motions may be stretched out.

The student should practice all beats at home in front of a mirror. If his beat seems awkward he may be sure he is not doing it correctly. The motion must be clear, precise, but effortless. The downbeat must move vertically down and — for the very first exercises at least — should start slightly above eye level.* It is difficult for any orchestra to follow a conductor who does not have a clear downbeat.

Fig. 5

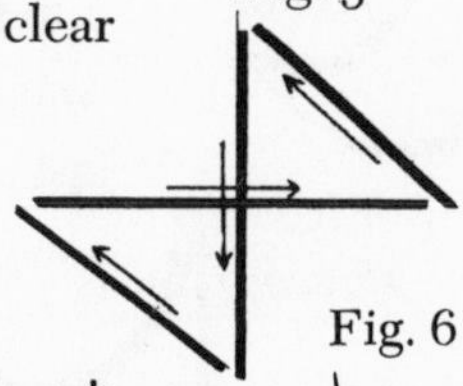

OTHER METERS

The beat-pattern used for the 2/4 meter is applicable to ¢ (alla breve) meter, and to 6/8 meter when it is too fast for six beats to a measure. Here the downbeat is on the first eighth and the upbeat on the fourth eighth.

The next basic beat is the 4/4 meter. The diagram for 4/4 meter is shown in Fig. 5.

Fig. 6 *legato*

The actual beat-pattern is Figs. 6, 7, and 8.

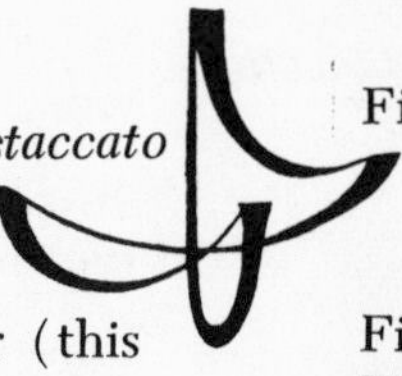

Fig. 7 *staccato*

The downbeat has the same "bounce" as in 2/4 meter (this should be the same for any meter), but all other beats are curved. The second beat should move clearly to the left; the third far out to the right; the last from there upward, with the curve to the left, to arrive at the spot where the first downbeat started. In 4/4 time, even more than in 2/4, a vague downbeat will be confusing. Fig. 9 is a *poor* beat-pattern, showing the *bad* habits a conductor may get into:

Fig. 8 *sharp staccato*

Fig. 9 *Incorrect*

* It is the *hand* that should start above eye level. Many conductors have dispensed with a baton, but for non-professional orchestras a baton is definitely advisable. It magnifies the most minute movement of the hand and its light color attracts more attention.

A baton is always held in the right hand. Left-handers will have to get used to doing this. Conducting is a two-handed skill, the left hand is an important accessory to the right, as will be seen later.

Fig. 10

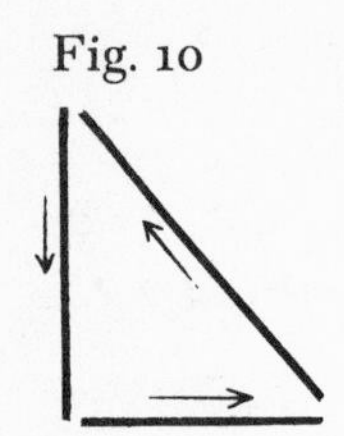

The 4/4 beat is, of course, also used for 4/8 meter, and for 12/8 meter when the latter is too fast to beat every eighth. This pattern is also used in 2/4 and ¢ time, when they are slow enough to make four beats advisable. Practice methods are the same as for 2/4 meter – as they are for all the beats below.

Fig. 11

legato

Fig. 12

staccato

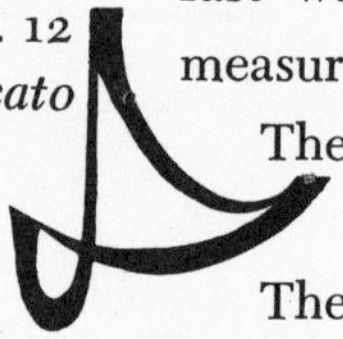

Fig. 13

sharp staccato

The 3/4 meter was originally a dance meter—sarabands, minuets, and waltzes are in 3/4 time – but it is now used for many different kinds of music. Both the *Star-Spangled Banner* and *America* are in 3/4 meter. (The Viennese waltz, and in fact all fast waltzes and most scherzos, are beaten in one beat to a measure.)

The basic diagram for 3/4 is shown in Fig. 10.

The actual beat-pattern is Figs. 11, 12, and 13.

The same beat is used for 3/8 meter (occurring frequently in slow movements of classical and early romantic symphonies), for 3/2 meter (unless it is in very slow tempo), and 9/8 meter in moderate or fast tempo.

The 6/8 meter is more complicated. Several beat-patterns for this meter are in use, but there is no good reason for the student to learn more than one when that one serves the purpose. The one described below, being the most logical, seems superior to any other. This meter is an extension of 4/8 meter, the first and third beat of which have been lengthened to double value. Consequently, 6/8 time is conducted like 4/8 (or 4/4) time, but with two beats in the same direction on the first and second as well as the fourth and fifth. Compare Figs. 14A and 14B.

Fig. 14

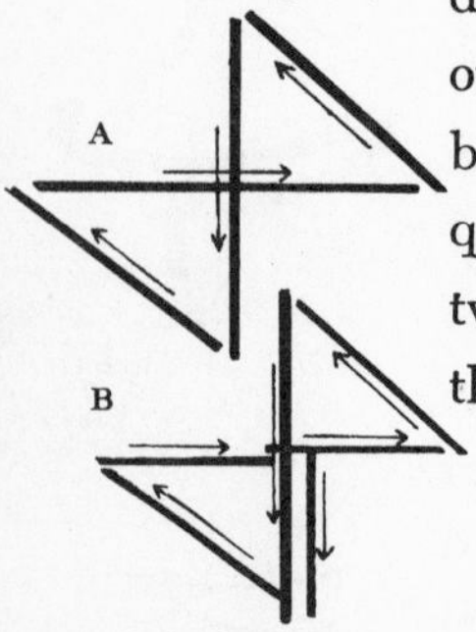

A

B

The actual beat-pattern is Fig. 15.

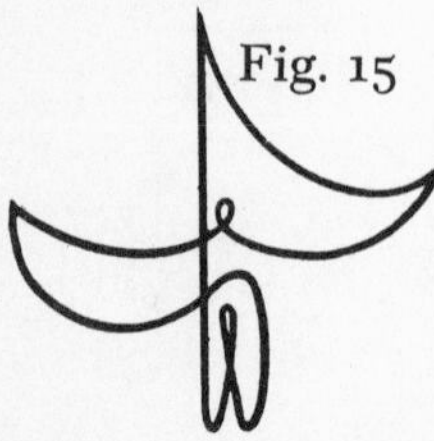

Fig. 15

(Staccato and legato beats are conducted as in 2/4, 4/4, and 3/4 meter, in this and all following beat-patterns.) The two vertical and two horizontal beats, following one another, create a certain problem for the beginner. He should exercise this beat until he feels completely relaxed doing it. Good working material: *Drink to Me Only with Thine Eyes, Silent Night,* and Mozart's Piano Sonata in A Major, K. 331 (beginning).

This beat is of course also used for 6/4 meter. Faster 6/8 (and 6/4) meter is beaten with two beats to the measure.

WALTZ BEAT

A single beat is used for waltzes (except slow ones). This beat, as simple as it seems to be, is not easy at all because it is so bare of mechanical and technical problems. A graceful technique helps produce a good performance.

The beat-pattern (showing the stress) is Fig. 16.

Fig. 16

The downbeat is fast and forceful – with a whipping motion – and bounces back with the elasticity prescribed for previous downbeats. It then continues upward much slower, just fast enough to arrive at the top for the start of the next measure. Use the first quarter for the downbeat and the other two quarters for the upbeat. At the end of this upbeat a flick of the wrist precedes the next downbeat. Care should be taken that the flow of movement never stops. To be effective, the waltz beat depends, more than any other, upon the conductor's freedom of motion. When it is done properly the lilt of the waltz should be evident, even without the sound of the orchestra.

The single beat is also used for fast 2/4 meter (finale of Mozart's *Prague* Symphony, K. 504; Turkish March from Beethoven's *Ruins of Athens*) and for most 3/4 time scherzos and fast minuets. In Beethoven's Fifth Symphony even the end of the finale (marked ¢) is done in single beats. The finale of Mozart's *Haffner* Symphony, K. 385, is also best conducted in single beats. All these one-beat meters are easier to execute than a waltz, either because they are faster, or because the two-part meter does not require the slight hesitation in the upward motion that is needed in a waltz.

SUBDIVISIONS

When the tempo is too slow, it may sometimes be advisable to subdivide beats. As a slow 2/4 meter may be conducted in four beats, so a slow 3/4 meter may have six; but it must never be conducted in the manner of 6/8 time, which consists of twice three eighths and not, as in this case, three times two. Consequently, the slow 3/4 or 3/2 meter is done as shown in Fig. 17

Fig. 17

A slow 4/4 or 4/2 meter with eight beats has the pattern as shown in Fig. 18.

Fig. 18

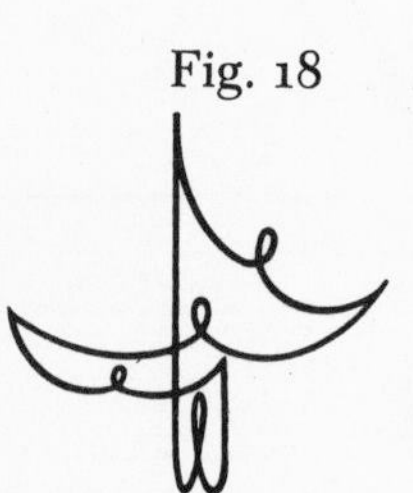

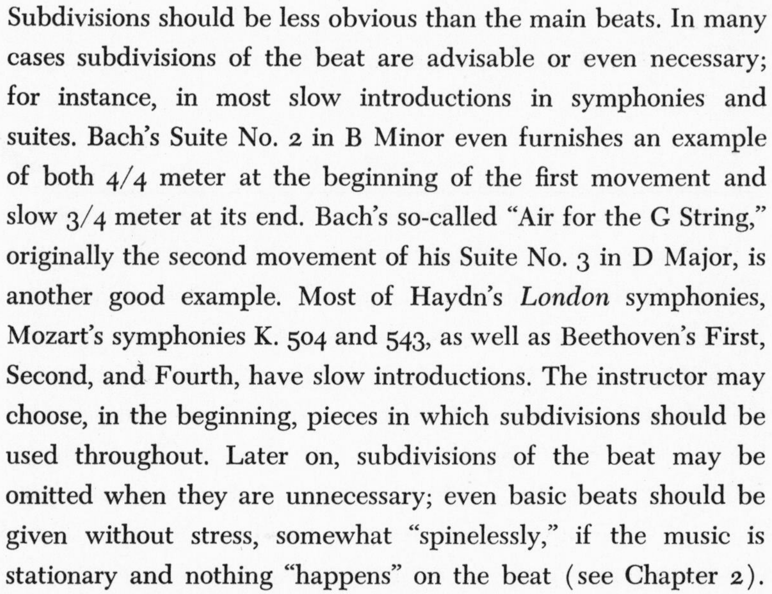

Subdivisions should be less obvious than the main beats. In many cases subdivisions of the beat are advisable or even necessary; for instance, in most slow introductions in symphonies and suites. Bach's Suite No. 2 in B Minor even furnishes an example of both 4/4 meter at the beginning of the first movement and slow 3/4 meter at its end. Bach's so-called "Air for the G String," originally the second movement of his Suite No. 3 in D Major, is another good example. Most of Haydn's *London* symphonies, Mozart's symphonies K. 504 and 543, as well as Beethoven's First, Second, and Fourth, have slow introductions. The instructor may choose, in the beginning, pieces in which subdivisions should be used throughout. Later on, subdivisions of the beat may be omitted when they are unnecessary; even basic beats should be given without stress, somewhat "spinelessly," if the music is stationary and nothing "happens" on the beat (see Chapter 2).

Fig. 19

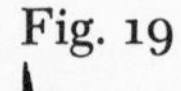

Slow 9/8 and 12/8 meters should also be beaten in eighths. The beat-patterns are Figs. 19 and 20.

Fig. 20

Ex. 1

Ex. 2

The most important beats have now been discussed. (The uneven beats – 5/4, 7/4 – occurring originally in Russian music and now in music of the twentieth century, are discussed in Chapter Eight.) It remains for the student to become thoroughly familiar with them. Practicing in front of a mirror will help. When the student has mastered the beat-patterns he has learned the "alphabet" of conducting.

2 Starts

Starting on the beat

IT IS no exaggeration to say that a student has mastered the most important manual problem of conducting when he is able to give a clear starting beat.

The very first motion of the conductor must define the exact moment and the exact tempo at which the orchestra is to start. The dynamic and expressive quality of the first notes, furthermore, will be strongly influenced by the vigor or softness of the conductor's motion.

PREPARATORY BEAT

The conductor must alert his players; the preparatory beat may be compared to taking a breath before singing, or – if a more vigorous start is required – to thrusting the arm back before throwing a ball. These are unconscious actions. The preparatory beat should become just such an action. A conductor need not even be aware of giving it. Students are likely to become so conscious of this preparatory beat that instead of executing it naturally, they precede it with an additional, unnecessary gesture. Thus, part of the orchestra may mistake the preparatory beat for the actual starting beat, and begin to play too early. (The terms "preparatory" and "starting" beat, used regularly from here on, should not be confused.)

The following rule applies to the execution of the preparatory beat: Use a full beat before the starting beat. The orthodox – and clearest – way of doing this is to give exactly the beat that precedes the starting beat, according to the patterns in Chapter One.

Some conductors – even of first-rate professional orchestras – have started the practice of conducting a full measure ahead. This may help to accomplish an accurate attack, but it "spoils" the orchestra. If the tempo changes suddenly, the conductor must use *one* preparatory beat to induce this sudden change. The orchestra will react more easily if it has become used to picking up the right tempo from the *one* preparatory beat at the start.

If a piece starts on a downbeat, the preparatory beat should be handled like an upbeat — that is, it moves from the right in a curve toward the top middle. This preparation should also be applied to 2/4 time, since the upbeat for this meter—with the slight hook at the beginning — would be awkward. The same holds true for single-beat measures, because the one beat consists of a down-and-up motion.

CONDUCTING

The student is now ready for actual conducting. Now he has to see if his motions bring about the desired effect, using his classmates as "guinea pigs." Start with singing by the class, even examples from orchestral literature. For this practice only a few measures need be sung, since all that is necessary is the start itself, in the right tempo and character. Every student in class should have a chance to conduct these few seconds, and quite a number of exercises can be handled by this method.* Whether conducting voices or instruments, the student must strive for the same goals: precision, musicianship, and clarity. If the voices do not start singing exactly together there is something wrong with the conductor's technique.

The student should always wait a few seconds before starting. If he lifts his baton and immediately gives the preparatory beat, his gesture may be mistaken for the actual beat. These few seconds give him a chance to glance over the orchestra and make sure that everybody is ready, and to prepare his mind for the tempo. He should sing the first measures silently to himself, then give the preparatory beat precisely.

The following example is an illustration.

Ex. 3

* For self-study and variety this singing may be substituted by piano playing. Singing is preferable, because the student conducts a group of persons who will have to react to his beat. Some of the examples from orchestral literature are practically not singable. Here the piano should be used. Naturally, not all examples mentioned lend themselves for exercises. They have been added for reference purposes.

EXERCISES

The exercises below have been compiled for basic practice in class (and at home in front of a mirror). They correspond to finger exercises for instrumentalists, and should assist in achieving the flexibility and authority needed for starting an orchestral work. Each beat-pattern has a staccato as well as legato version. The exercises should be done in different tempos and dynamics; the class should not know in advance which speed and volume the student conductor has chosen.

START ON DOWNBEAT

When the first note is forte, the preparatory beat must be

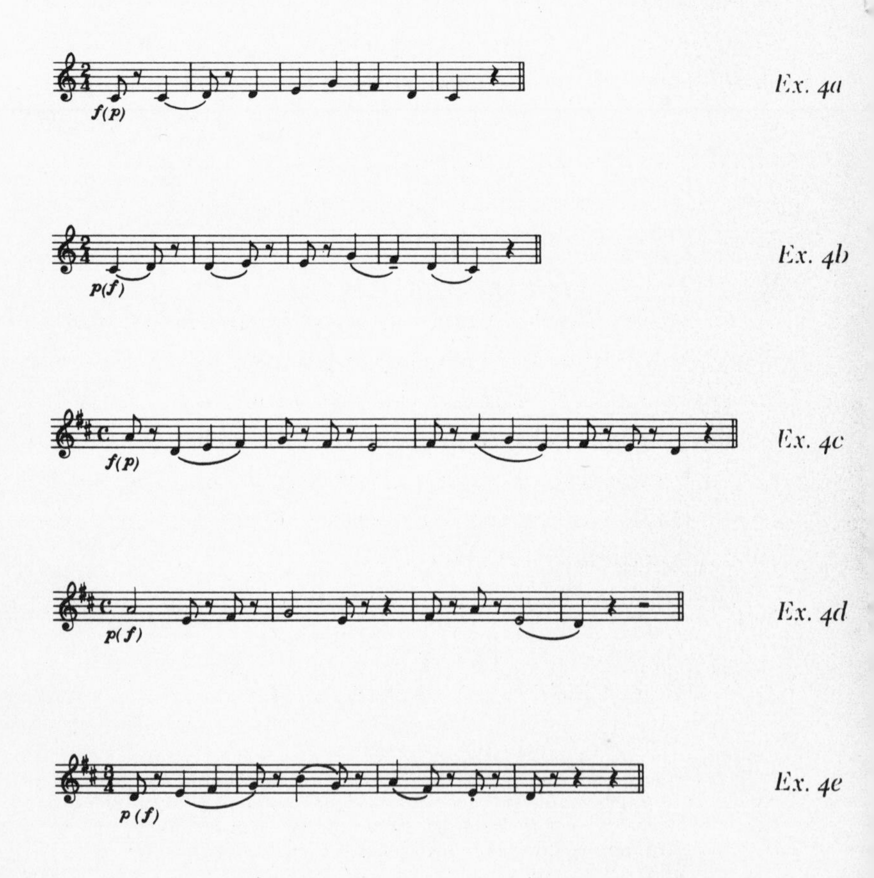

forceful; when the piece starts softly, the preparation should indicate it. A staccato entrance should be preceded by a sharp beat; when the staccato is soft, a flick of the wrist will suffice. An intermediate beat also requires a rather sharp motion, depending upon the volume required for the first note. For a soft, slow legato entrance, the conductor should give an almost "spineless" preparation; the actual start of the orchestra should not occur before the downbeat reaches bottom, just before bouncing back. (Disregard the last note in each pattern. These will be treated in the following chapter.)

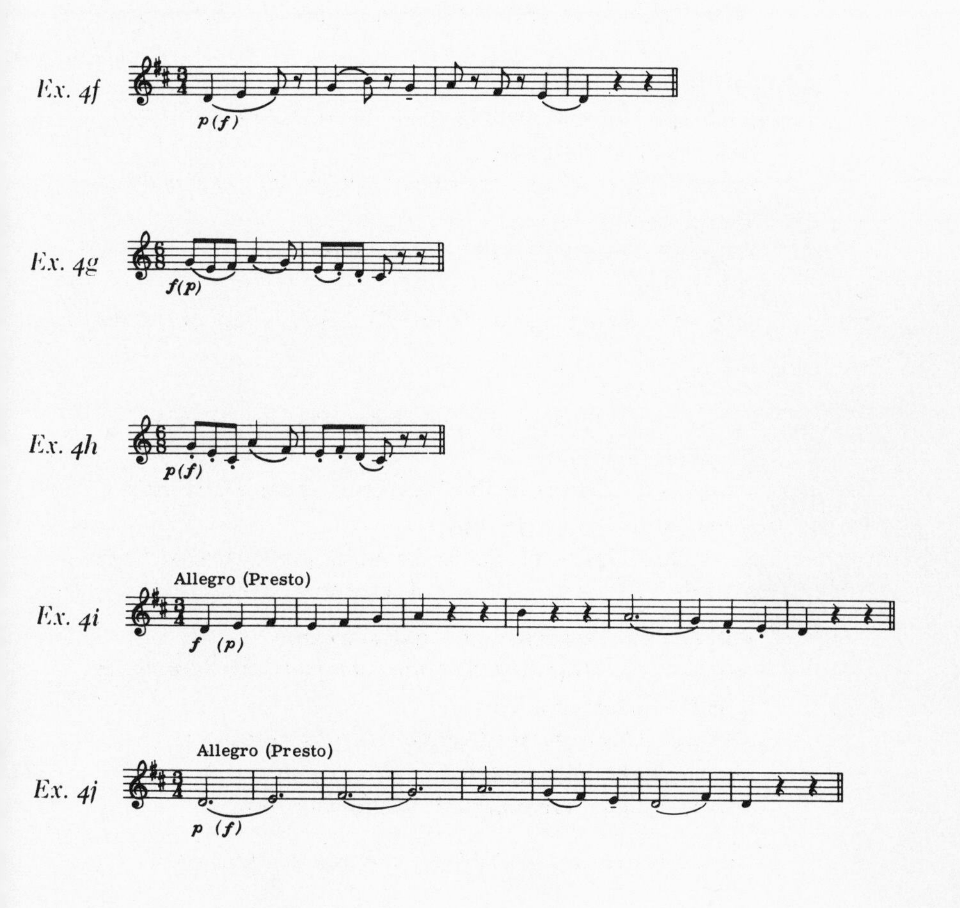

EXAMPLES

The list of musical examples on the following pages is an extensive one, although most students are likely to have access to only a few of the works mentioned. Selections might be copied on the blackboard or mimeographed (only the melodic line is needed), thus giving each student a chance to conduct while the class sings.

two beats:

2/4 Light, intermediate:
Twinkle, Twinkle, Little Star.
Staccato, with a lilt:
BIZET: Habanera, from *Carmen* (start the accompaniment).#*
Soft staccato, faster:
SCHUBERT: Second ballet music, from *Rosamunde*.#
Soft, intermediate, slow:
BRAHMS: Theme, in *Variations on a Theme by Haydn*.#
Sharp, strong, faster:
STRAUSS: Overture to *The Gypsy Baron*.#
Still faster (staccato):
MOZART: Osmin's aria, from *The Abduction from the Seraglio*.#
More forceful:
STRAVINSKY: Russian Dance, from *Petroushka*.#
Very soft, legato:
STRAVINSKY: Dance of the Princesses, from *The Firebird.*
Strong staccato (pizzicato):
DE FALLA: Dance of Terror, from *El Amor Brujo.* (The pattern: Allegro [rhythm] *etc.* Try it clapping hands.)

(alla breve) ¢ Rather fast (intermediate and staccato):
MOZART: Overture to *The Abduction from the Seraglio*.#
Slightly faster, smoother:
MOZART: Overture to *The Marriage of Figaro*.#
Slower, light but smooth:
MENDELSSOHN: Opening of Violin Concerto.#

* The # sign applies to pieces suitable for exercises in Chapter One.

Very clear, sharp:
WAGNER: Beginning of Act Two of *Tannhäuser*.#*
Forceful, majestic (intermediate and staccato):
BEETHOVEN: Finale of Fifth Symphony.#

6/8 Intermediate:
Three Blind Mice.
Legato, with a lilt:
OFFENBACH: Barcarole, from *Tales of Hoffmann*.#
Light (staccato), not fast:
MOZART: Serenade, from *Don Giovanni* (mandolin).#

6/4 Slow, legato:
BLOM: *Still as the Night.*

6/16 Very light and fast:
BIZET: Quintet from *Carmen*.#

four beats:

4/4 Broad forte staccato; then soft legato:
HAYDN: Beginning of Symphony No. 98.#
Forceful, intermediate:
SCHUBERT: Beginning of Ninth Symphony.
Similar:
HANDEL: *Glory to God,* from *Messiah.*
Sharper (intermediate and staccato):
MOZART: Beginning of *Eine Kleine Nachtmusik*.#
Light (staccato):
TCHAIKOVSKY: March, from *Nutcracker suite*.#
Intermediate (clear preparation for every half note):
TCHAIKOVSKY: Beginning of *Romeo and Juliet* overture.
Broad, legato with slightly marked attacks:
HANDEL: Funeral March from *Saul*.#
Not so slow, smoother:
HUMPERDINCK: Overture to *Hänsel and Gretel*.#

4/8 Moderately fast, staccato:
SCHUBERT: Second movement of Ninth Symphony.#

¢ Forceful, at entrance of voice lighter (intermediate):
MOZART: Duet from *Marriage of Figaro* (No. 19).#

* Because of the fast sextuplets the start requires exact preparation.

2/4 Light, almost staccato:
HAYDN: Andante of *London* Symphony (102).#
Fast, staccato (pizzicato):
GLUCK: Dance from *At the Court of Maria Theresa* #* (may be done in two beats).

12/8 Slow, mostly legato:
HANDEL: *Pastoral Symphony*, from *Messiah* (also in twelve beats).#
Slow, molto legato:
BACH: First chorus in *St. Matthew Passion.*#
Slightly faster:
BACH: *Sanctus*, from B Minor Mass.#
Still faster (almost intermediate):
BEETHOVEN: Second movement of *Pastoral* Symphony.#

three beats:

3/4 Intermediate: *America.*
Broad, not too slow (intermediate legato):
✓HANDEL: *Largo.*#
Moderate legato:
✓WAGNER: *Preis-Lied* from *Die Meistersinger.*#
Very slow, legato:
MASCAGNI: *Intermezzo Sinfonico*, from *Cavalleria Rusticana.*#
Intermediate, almost staccato, slowly spaced:
✓MOZART: Minuet from *Don Giovanni.*#
Somewhat similar:
✓BRAHMS: Third movement of Second Symphony.#
Much faster, staccato:
MOZART: Figaro's cavatina, from *The Marriage of Figaro.*#
Sharper:
BIZET: Carillon from *L'Arlésienne* suite.
Fast, some staccato, some intermediate:
STRAVINSKY: Beginning of *Petroushka.*#
Smooth, with a lilt:
TCHAIKOVSKY: Third movement of Fifth Symphony.#

* A suite of pieces from Gluck's *Don Juan*, published by G. Schirmer Inc.

3/8 Intermediate legato, smooth:
BEETHOVEN: Second movement of Second Symphony.#

Legato and staccato (light):
HANDEL: Minuets from *Water Music.*#

2
Starts

Intermediate legato (smooth but clear):
BACH: First alto solo from *St. Matthew Passion.*

Almost staccato, forte:
BACH: Gloria from *B Minor Mass.*

3/2 Intermediate, sharp:
HANDEL: Hornpipe from Concerto Grosso No. 7.#

Similar (more forceful):
HANDEL: Hornpipe from *Water Music.*#

Very slow (intermediate legato):
BUSONI: Cortège from *Doctor Faust* (saraband).

9/8 Legato:
FOSTER: *Beautiful Dreamer.*

Legato:
BACH: *Jesu, Joy of Man's Desiring.*#

Marcato, intermediate:
WAGNER: Siegmund's Song from *Die Walküre.*#

six beats:

6/8 Intermediate:
ARNE: *Drink to Me Only with Thine Eyes.*

Legato:
GRUBER: *Silent Night.*

6/4 Soft legato:
SCHUMANN: Beginning of Second Symphony.#

Sustained but staccato (pizzicato):
BRUCKNER: Adagio from Fifth Symphony.#

one beat:

3/4 Smooth waltz (intermediate legato):
Daisy, Daisy.

Same (slightly more legato):
LEHAR: Waltz from *Merry Widow.*

Sharp intermediate staccato:
BEETHOVEN: Minuet from Second Symphony.#

Slower, heavier, more staccato:
BRUCKNER: Scherzo of Sixth Symphony.

3/8 Staccato (very light):
MENDELSSOHN: Scherzo from *Midsummer Night's Dream.*#

2/4 Similar:
MOZART: Finale of *Prague* Symphony K. 504.#
Similar (slightly slower):
MOZART: Finale of Symphony No. 33, K. 318.#
Sharper:
MOZART: Champagne aria from *Don Giovanni.*#

2/8 Very sharp, staccato:
PUCCINI: Beginning of Act II of *La Bohème.*#

six beats (three with subdivision):

3/4 Smooth legato:
BACH: Adagio from Piano Concerto in D Minor.

eight beats (four with subdivision):

4/4 Light staccato (moderate tempo):
WEBER: *Oberon* overture (at measure 10).
Legato melody, bass almost staccato:
BACH: *Air for G String* (from Third Suite).#

nine beats:

9/8 Legato and staccato:
See Example One.
Legato:
DEBUSSY: *Afternoon of a Faun* ("spineless" beats).#

twelve beats:

12/8 Legato and pizzicato (intermediate):
STRAVINSKY: Beginning of *The Firebird.*#
Legato and staccato:
See Example Two.

Legato:
DEBUSSY: Last four measures (horns) of *Afternoon of a Faun.*

When the same excerpt is done many times the tempo should occasionally be changed — even to a "wrong" tempo — although this requires skill from the conductor.

It is not always possible to make definite recommendations as to the style of a beat. In many examples some instruments play staccato, others legato; or matters may change quickly within a piece. The conductor must always be flexible.

START ON UPBEAT *(pick-up)*

For starting a piece on an upbeat the beat-patterns of Chapter One should be followed. In 2/4 or alla breve meter the downbeat will be the preparatory beat. Start at the top, hold the baton high, then drop it as for any downbeat. For all other meters the preparatory beat starts left and moves right. One-beat measures, because they consist only of downbeats, do not belong in this category.

EXAMPLES

In order to acquaint students with as much of the literature as possible this list begins with three excerpts.

second beat:

2/4 Legato:
VERDI: *Otello,* last act, Willow song.

Ex. 5a

¢ Partly legato, partly staccato:
BACH: Suite in B Minor.

6/8 MOZART's *Figaro,* Act Three chorus

2/4 Light intermediate:
HAYDN: Finale of Symphony No. 88 (see also allegro, first movement).#

4/4 Light staccato (wrist):
MOZART: Opening scene of *Don Giovanni.*#

6/8 Vigorous staccato, not too fast:
GLUCK: Finale of *At the Court of Maria Theresa.*
Similar but soft:
HAYDN: First allegros in *Surprise* and *Drum Roll* Symphonies

fourth beat:

4/4 Staccato upbeat:
SCHUMANN: Beginning of First Symphony.

Andante un poco maestoso

f

Ex. 6a

2/4 In four beats,
Intermediate:
HAYDN: Symphony No. 103, andante

Ex. 6b

4/4 Intermediate:
Auld Lang Syne.
Forceful, majestic, intermediate:
BRAHMS: Main theme, finale of First Symphony.#
Similar, slightly faster:
Oh Come All Ye Faithful.
Broad, intermediate legato:
BACH: Chorales from *St. Matthew Passion.*
Light, intermediate:
MENDELSSOHN: Third movement of Violin Concerto.#

2/4 Intermediate but clear:
BEETHOVEN: Funeral march from Eroica Symphony.
Staccato-legato:
HAYDN: Andante from *Drum Roll* Symphony.#

third beat:

3/4 Legato, intermediate:
WAGNER: Pilgrims' Chorus from *Tannhäuser.*

Ex. 7
Andante maestoso
p

Staccato:
HAYDN: Symphony No. 95, minuet.
Intermediate:
The Star-Spangled Banner.
Soft, legato:
BACH: Soprano aria Part Two, *St. Matthew Passion* (Flute and English horns).#
Slower, similar (four sixteenths in pickup):
MAHLER: Second movement of Ninth Symphony.#

3/8 Staccato and legato, small beats:
BEETHOVEN: Second movement of First Symphony.#
Intermediate legato (light):
BEETHOVEN: Second movement of Fifth Symphony.#

9/8 Intermediate legato:
Down in the Valley.

sixth beat:

6/8 Intermediate:
BEETHOVEN: Quartet from *Fidelio.*

Andante sostenuto (in 6)

p

Ex. 8

MOZART: Second movement of Symphony in G Minor.#
Somewhat more legato:
SCHUBERT: Second movement of Fifth Symphony.#
Light staccato, not slow:
GLUCK: Siciliana from *At the Court of Maria Theresa.*
Slow, legato:
WAGNER: Prelude to *Tristan and Isolde.*
(After "spineless" beats in the first measure, the sixth beat will need preparation.)#

START TWO BEATS BEFORE BARLINE

The start in 4/4 time is on the third, or horizontal beat. Students sometimes feel awkward doing the preparation from middle to left. Visualize an imaginary line across a blackboard: to start such a line one automatically moves the hand to the left. This automatic motion is exactly what is needed as a preparatory beat for the horizontal (slightly curved) starting beat. Care should be taken that this preparatory beat is done exactly in the tempo of the two following beats.

In 3/4 time the preparatory beat will be the downbeat (like the downbeat for 2/4 time, when starting on the last beat).

In 6/8 time the preparatory beat must start (according to the chart) from far left and should not go beyond the middle, since the starting beat moves in the same direction. Some conductors prefer the beat-pattern shown in Fig. 21 since the two beats before the barline may be considered two upbeats.

Fig. 21

EXAMPLES

In the following, style and tempo are *not* indicated:

(in four),
MOZART: Aria No. 15 from *Abduction from the Seraglio.*

Ex. 9 Adagio (in 4)

4/4 HANDEL: Gavotte from Concerto Grosso No. 7 (with oboes).
GLUCK: Gavotte from *Iphigenia in Aulis.*

2/4 MOZART: *Batti, Batti,* from *Don Giovanni.* (Four beats).#

3/4 GLUCK: Chaconne from *Iphigenia in Aulis.*#

¢ MOZART: Andante from *Eine Kleine Nachtmusik.*#

6/8 RIMSKY-KORSAKOV: The Prince and the Princess, from Scheherazade. (This may later switch to two beats a measure.)

START THREE BEATS BEFORE BARLINE

This applies mainly to 4/4 and 6/8 meter. In 4/4 the starting beat is the second beat, with the downbeat as preparation. In 6/8 meter the fourth beat will be the starting beat – that moves from far left toward the middle. Here too an imaginary horizontal line in the air will help.

(legato) VERDI: *Otello,* Act IV

4/4 GLUCK: Overture to *Iphigenia in Aulis.*
HANDEL: Grave from Concerto Grosso No. 8.
VERDI: First scene of *Aida.*
MAHLER: Last movement of Ninth Symphony.

6/8 (legato) VERDI: *Otello,* Act II, Iago's accusation.

Andantino (in 6)

Ex. 11

Further Examples.

Ex. 12a

Ex. 12b

START ON SECOND AND THIRD BEATS IN 6/8 TIME

A conductor will rarely have a chance to apply this beat but they are included here in order to cover all possibilities. If the beat-patterns in Chapter One are carefully followed, these beats should cause no difficulty:

Ex. 13a

Ex. 13b

Ex. 14a

Ex. 14b

STARTS ON RESTS

A composer will frequently facilitate a precise start by adding rests before the start. These rests must be beaten (with no preparation) if the players, especially those who do not play at the start, are not to be confused. When the printed rest coincides with the preparatory beat, it will of course be disregarded.

EXAMPLES

The following excerpts are from BIZET: *L'Arlésienne* suite.

HAYDN: Last movement of Symphony No. 86.
SCHUMANN: Finale of First Symphony.
WAGNER: Introduction to Act Three of *Tannhäuser*.

Opening measures of:

VERDI: *Otello*. (Especially interesting.)
MOUSSORGSKY: *Khovantchina*.
BACH: *Et Resurexit* from B Minor Mass.
PUCCINI: Second act of *Tosca*.
PUCCINI: Act II of *Madama Butterfly*.
DVOŘÁK: Adagio of Fourth Symphony.
DVOŘÁK: Third movement of Fourth Symphony.

Some of the above properly belong to the next part of this chapter. By beating the printed rests, however, the problem of starting between beats is eliminated.

Starting between beats

Very often the first note of a piece will not coincide with the conductor's beat. The offbeat beginning may be an eighth, a sixteenth, even a thirty-second, and often it is more than one note. In these cases, the following rule applies:

If a piece starts within beats, prepare for the beat *following* the offbeat note or notes; actually, disregard them. If this rule sounds strange the best way to prove it is by experiment. The class might sing and a student conduct the following phrase:

Ex. 17a

and then the Marseillaise:

Ex. 17b

It should become evident that the same beat achieves the desired result.

Offbeat notes may occur before a downbeat, an upbeat, or any other beat. The following exercise from *The Marriage of Figaro* should be done in 4/4 and alla breve time as indicated:

Andante ♩= 72-120 𝅗𝅥= 48-88

Ex. 18

For practicing an offbeat upbeat in 6/8 time the following example from *The Magic Flute* should be used:

Allegro 60-96

Ex. 19

A staccato upbeat in *slow* 4/4 time is more difficult. The preparatory beat must be clear and sharp even for soft attacks, much sharper than the preparatory beat for a piece that starts on a strong staccato downbeat. In fast alla breve time, the offbeat notes constitute no problem – there is no difference whether they are loud or soft, staccato or legato. They occur almost simultaneously with the downbeat, just before it reaches the end.

EXAMPLES

Here are examples of a single offbeat note before the downbeat:

2/4 *The Farmer in the Dell.*

BEETHOVEN: Finale of *Prometheus* (later used in the Eroica).#

BARTOK: Allegro from Music for Strings, Percussion, and Celesta (pizzicato).#

¢ BRAHMS: Beginning of Fourth Symphony.

4/4 FOSTER: *My Old Kentucky Home.*

SCHUMANN: *The Happy Farmer.*

2/4 (Four beats.)

MOZART: *Dies Bildnis ist bezaubernd schön,* from *Magic Flute.*

12/8 (Four beats.)

HANDEL: *He shall feed his Flock,* from *Messiah.*

6/8 *For He's a Jolly Good Fellow.*

SCHUMANN: *The Wild Horseman.*

BACH: Duet from Cantata, *Sleepers Awake.*

3/4 HAYDN: Beginning of Symphony No. 88 (A sixteenth upbeat in slow tempo, often played too fast.)

ROSSINI: *Barber of Seville* Overture (4/4). (The above is true here, too.)

GLUCK: Minuet from *At the Court of Maria Theresa.*

9/8 WAGNER: Start of Act II of *Die Walküre.*

3/4 (One beat.)

My Bonnie Lies Over the Ocean.

BEETHOVEN: Minuet from First Symphony, scherzos from most other symphonies.#

SCHUMANN: Scherzo from First Symphony.

offbeat notes before other beats

EXERCISES

BEETHOVEN: Last duet from *Fidelio.*

Allegro vivace (in 2)

Ex. 20

BIZET: Card aria from *Carmen.*

Andante molto moderato (♩= 66)

Ex. 21

4/4 The *Marseillaise.*

¢ MOZART: Last movement of D Minor Piano Concerto.

2/4 BACH: Last movement of *Brandenburg* Concerto No. 5.
TCHAIKOVSKY: Second movement of Fourth Symphony.

3/4 GRIEG: *I Love Thee.*
Londonderry Air.
HANDEL: Loure from *Water Music.*
MOZART: Minuet from Symphony No. 29.

two notes preceding starting note

This should not create a problem, especially if the two notes are fast and closely attached to the starting-beat note. Try *Dixie* as a practice exercise.

MOZART: Papageno-Papagena Duet from *Magic Flute.*

VERDI: *Sempre Libera* from *Traviata.*

Dark Eyes.

2/4 MOZART: Finale of Symphony No. 39.
MOZART: Susanna's aria (No. 12), from *Marriage of Figaro.*
FOSTER: *Oh, Susanna.*

¢ MAHLER: Rondo-Burleske from Ninth Symphony.

4/4 BEETHOVEN: Leonora's aria, from *Fidelio,* Act 2.

6/8 HAYDN: Finale of Symphony No. 98.
MENDELSSOHN: Allegro in finale of *Scottish* Symphony
MOZART: No. 9 in *Les Petits Riens.*

3/4 BACH: Last movement of Double Concerto (two violins).

2/4 (*In one.*) SCHUBERT: Finale of Ninth Symphony.

Students will notice, when practicing these examples, that some two-note patterns are easier than one. It depends, as in the exercise at the beginning of this section, on the tempo and character of the piece. The slower the tempo the harder it is to achieve the offbeat notes accurately. Here, too, it is a question of how close they are to the starting beat.

Up to now all conducting action has been limited to the hand. Sometimes, however, a nod of the head can be reassuring, since it heightens the players' confidence in entering on time. The head is lifted slightly for the notes preceding the beat, then moves downward *with* the beat. But this head motion may not suit every student, and as one of the subtleties of conducting it is more of an accessory than a necessity.

When a piece starts between beats, there must be a certain give and take between conductor and orchestra. If the conductor's preparatory beat is unclear, the orchestra will not start at the right moment or play the offbeat notes in the tempo he wants. The conductor must not beat the starting beat until the orchestra has exactly reached it. A sensitive ear is needed for this.

Even greater sensitivity is needed when more than two notes precede the starting beat. Many a conductor resorts to two preparatory beats – but this should seldom be necessary if he has a feel for what he is doing.

The following example, with three offbeat notes, should be done by every student. It is the start of Mahler's Fifth Symphony:

Ex. 25

Additional examples:

BRAHMS: First Scherzo from Serenade No. 1.

Ex. 26

MOZART: Queen of the Night aria from *Magic Flute.*

Allegro assai (in two)

Ex. 27

BEETHOVEN: First vocal piece in *Fidelio.*

BERLIOZ: Hungarian March, in *Damnation of Faust.*

SCHUBERT: Main theme, first movement, *Tragic* Symphony.

R. STRAUSS: Beginning of *Don Juan* (difficult).

MAHLER: Fifth movement of Second Symphony.

The main theme of the overture to Gluck's *Iphigenia in Aulis* occurs during the course of the piece, but could be used as a beginning. Act III of Wagner's *Die Walküre* starts with a four thirty-second note upbeat in 9/8 time. These should be like the lash of a whip, with no problem in beating because they are so closely attached to the first downbeat.

In the finale of Mozart's *Eine kleine Nachtmusik* three offbeat notes constitute an important part of the thematic material; they start the actual theme. When the downbeat occurs a part of this theme has already been played: if not stated clearly the listener may be unable to grasp its meaning. Consequently even experienced conductors give a slight, almost unnoticeable downbeat before the preparatory beat.

The opening of Beethoven's Fifth Symphony has vexed conductors since it was written. It starts on three eighths before the first downbeat (with one beat to the measure in 2/4 meter). These preliminary notes constitute the main part of the theme. To achieve perfect accuracy, it is best to follow this procedure: Begin with the hand ready for the start; in exactly the time of one beat (one measure) retract it slightly; after this motion thrust the arm forward for a vigorous down beat.

At the start of Puccini's opera, *La Bohéme,* there is the similar problem of 3/8 meter beaten in one. The first measure starts with a sixteenth rest, then a sixteenth note, followed by two eighths. Again it is best to retract the hand one measure, before thrusting it forward for the first downbeat.

This chapter has provided the student with many examples. Since the starting beat is almost the chief problem in conducting technique the student should study as many as possible. It is even of further advantage if he supplements the examples in this book with additional ones, which he can find throughout standard and modern music literature.

3 Endings and pauses

The ending beat

A PIECE may end in different ways:

1] Fade-out. The last note is held for a full measure or longer (often with an added fermata). In romantic music the last measures are frequently marked ritardando.

2] Crescendo, followed by fading out: < >

3] Short notes, generally loud in an allegro, soft in an adagio. Here, too, a ritardando may occur, especially in a slow, soft ending.

4] An abrupt stop at the end of the last note. This usually occurs when the final note is held, often with an added crescendo, at full strength for a certain length.

FADE-OUT

When the ending consists of a single note or chord held for a full measure or longer, do not give every beat. Conduct the first beat of the chord, let the baton bounce back to eye level, then gradually lower it for the diminuendo. To stop the orchestra, give another very subtle downbeat, perhaps with a small preparation. The last note should be held exactly as long as its value requires. In order to create the impression that the tone is still lingering somewhere in the air do not set down the baton immediately. These fade-outs can be very effective.*

EXERCISE:

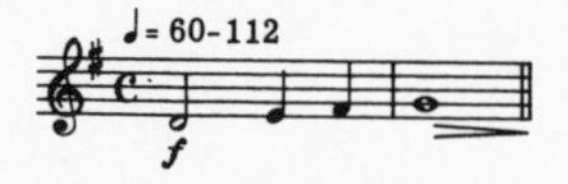

Ex. 28

Examples:

SCHUBERT: First movement of *Unfinished* Symphony.
SCHUBERT: Last movement of Ninth Symphony.

* If the last measure has no diminuendo but is piano throughout, the procedure is similar; the lowering of the baton, however, is not needed.

BEETHOVEN: Second movement of Second Symphony.
DVOŘÁK: Finale of *New World* Symphony.
PUCCINI: End of *La Bohème.*
WAGNER: End of *Götterdämmerung.*

CRESCENDO

When the last fade-out is preceded by a crescendo, lift the arms—here the use of both arms may be appropriate—then lower them. The dynamic climax should take place exactly where the composer intended it.

EXERCISE:

Ex. 29

♩ = 54-104

p

Examples:

SCHUBERT: Second movement of Ninth Symphony.
SCHUBERT: Second movement of *Unfinished* Symphony.
MOUSSORGSKY: Act I, Act III, and first tableau of Act IV of *Khovantchina.*
WAGNER: End of *Tristan and Isolde.*

The end of the third movement of Brahms's First Symphony and the end of the first movement of his Second are similar, but not exactly the same. Find the problem in each case. (There is a slight modification in the second.)

ENDINGS WITH SHORT NOTES

When the last measures have strong, short notes, in fast tempo, the beat should continue in the usual patterns to the very end, with a slight emphasis on the very last note. Since this is generally a downbeat it will end at the bottom, where it should stay for just a few seconds. Most fast movements in Haydn and Beethoven finish this way, but Mozart's allegro movements have more diversified endings, often with fermatas. His E-flat major symphony, K. 543, is unusual in that it closes on an upbeat (2/4 time). Instead of giving this beat in the usual pattern it is advisable to use another downbeat – thus having two downbeats in this measure. Dvorák's Fourth Symphony has a similar ending.

When slow movements end on a soft staccato note, as in Haydn's Symphony No. 88 and Beethoven's Second, the regular beat should be continued to the last note. The final beat should be given very lightly.

EXERCISE:

Ex. 30

CUTTING OFF A HELD NOTE

When a note, often increased dynamically, is to be abruptly stopped one uses a "cutoff," which may be accomplished in different ways. While holding the last note, the baton should be moved slowly to the upper right. Cut off with a quick circular motion to bottom center, somewhat like a figure six. Or stay in the center, and cut off as if crossing out the last note. Either cutoff is good: the student should choose the one he considers most suitable.

EXERCISE:

♩= 116-152 𝅗𝅥=84-112

f

Ex. 31

When the last measure is exactly a whole note long, cut off with the downbeat that would follow the concluding measure. Examples can be found in a large number of works by Handel, as well as in the overture to Weber's *Der Freischütz* and the overture to Wagner's *Tannhäuser.*

When the last note is less than a full measure long, a very clear cutoff-beat is needed. A sluggishly played final note can spoil the effect of a whole performance. At the ends of Haydn's Symphonies No. 103 and 104, and Mozart's *Haffner* and G minor Symphonies (K. 385 and 550), the final notes are half notes in alla breve time. Consequently, the cutoff-beat – up to which the last note should be held – will be an upbeat. It can be conducted like any regular cutoff or like an upside-down six.

A similar procedure applies to endings of slow movements. If the beat is in eighths and the last note (on the downbeat) is one eighth long, the note must be held a full beat and cut off on the second beat. The dynamic quality of the ending should determine if the cutoff is to be short and fast or slower and more tender.

The slow movements of Mozart's Symphonies in D, K. 504; in E-flat, K. 543; in G Minor, K. 550; in C, K. 551; are all good examples. In the latter two cases the final beat is not a downbeat, but the same rule applies. The cutoff should occur on the beat following the final note.

In the slow movement of Beethoven's First Symphony, the last note fills one quarter. It should be held two eighths and cut off on the third.

In the second movement of his Third Symphony, Mahler especially requires that the last half note be done strictly in time (and with no ritardando). As an experienced craftsman he knew how often conductors and orchestras overlook such details.

Often a piece ends softly, but is finally cut off by a sudden blast of the full orchestra. Then the last beat must have an especially sharp preparation. Such dramatic endings occur frequently in opera:

WAGNER: Act IV of *Rienzi;* Act II of *Siegfried;* Act II of *Die Meistersinger.*
MOZART: Trio No. 13 in *Marriage of Figaro* (with an upbeat).
BIZET: Trio in Act III of *Carmen.*
VERDI: Ulrica's aria *Un Ballo in Maschera.*
BEETHOVEN: Finale of *Pastoral* Symphony (with upbeat).

It often happens that a cutoff is required at a place other than the end of the piece. Such a cutoff will be sharper after a strong note than after a soft one. The following exercise illustrates both. (It also gives the student an opportunity to use the "spineless" beats mentioned in Chapter 1.)

Ex. 32

This exercise should be done slowly, ♩ about 60, and then faster, 𝅗𝅥 about 80. Any other tempo within this range may also be used. The conductor will have to announce the number of beats, two or four.

When done in four beats, the third beat in measure 1 should be a rather sharp cutoff. Though the fourth beat is "dead," it must be used here as preparation for the soft first piano note in measure 2. It should be "tender." The first note in measure 2 is also a sustained beat: tenuto. Carry the baton through the full beat. The second beat is used for a cutoff (a soft one), while the third beat should be a staccato preparation for the sharp staccato upbeat. The downbeat in measure 3 is strong, but considering the following diminuendo and the fact that nothing "happens" on the other beats, the beats should become more and more "spineless." The last beat is a soft preparation for measure 4. In this measure the second beat is "spineless," the third a *soft* cutoff. The fourth beat is a soft staccato preparation for the next note. In measure 6, soft staccato beats on one and three, but two and four should be rather "spineless." Measure 7 grows in intensity but again nothing "happens"; the beats on two and three should flow into each other without being stressed as single beats. The last beat should be sharp, as preparation for the staccato downbeat, which should be short. No further beats are needed in measure 8.

When done in two beats, the procedure is different, but it should not be difficult for the student to solve on the basis of what he has now learned.

The fermata

Holding a fermata (pause) is no problem, but there are different ways of ending it. The question is whether or not to cut it off entirely. If not, it can be connected to the following note, or – more often – can be followed by enough time for taking a breath.

The difference between the two methods can be illustrated in the last part of the *Star-Spangled Banner*. In the passage "Oh say, does that star-spangled banner yet wave," there is a fermata on "wave." Some conductors cut this fermata off with the same cutoff used for ending a piece, then start afresh with a preparatory beat for the phrase "o'er the land of the free." Others use the cutoff itself as a preparation beat. In the latter method one stops on the second beat for the required hold without moving too far toward the right; there must be enough space left to continue in the same direction.

Each student should practice both methods – an especially simple procedure since everybody knows the *Star-Spangled Banner*. If the class is attentive and the conductor's beat is clear, there should be no trouble following him exactly.

There is no rule about which fermata should be cut off and which should not. The *Star-Spangled Banner* shows that both beats can be used; the choice is a matter of taste. More often than not, however, it is musically more convincing not to cut off. As to the *length* of the fermata, it is generally held about twice as long as the value of the note to which it applies. The composer sometimes specifies an especially long fermata by marking it *lunga* ("long").

Use examples 28 and 29 (on pages 30 and 31) as exercises with a fermata on the last note.

FERMATAS IN BEETHOVEN'S FIFTH SYMPHONY

The two thematic statements at the beginning of the work stand by themselves, each with a fermata. Since these are unattached to a following passage it seems appropriate that each fermata be cut off. After the first cutoff only a sharp downbeat is needed to start the next pattern. No preparation is necessary, since the tempo has already been established. In the second instance an extra measure is added to the fermata measure, indicating a slightly longer hold. After the cutoff of this fermata, a further downbeat, this one very subtle (but precise) should induce the second violins to start their next attack clearly—but softly.

If only a short interruption is desired—and this is appropriate for the return of the theme in the recapitulation—the cutoff of the first fermata should be used as preparation for the next downbeat; the interruption would be no longer than one (short) measure (one beat), thus enhancing the climax. When the same passage occurs in the coda no interruption at all is suggested. The fermata will be cut off by the downbeat for the following attack. Always cut off the second fermata, followed by a soft passage. (See Part Four.)

SHIFT OF FERMATA

BEETHOVEN: Last movement of Eighth Symphony:

Ex. 33

In the example above it is best to shift the fermatas and place them on the barline. The conductor moves his baton sharply upward on the second beat for the forte in the basses; the shift of the fermatas will cause him to remain at the top for the pause. The following downbeat, which prepares the first time for the entrance of strings and winds and the second for the second violins, must be very clear but small because of the pianissimo. Adhering to the letter of the score would require one downbeat for the fermata, another as preparatory beat for the second half of the measure. Obviously the suggested shift allows a simpler and clearer beat, without changing Beethoven's music in any way.

In Beethoven's *Egmont* overture the sustained first note fades out. At first, therefore, hold the fermata full strength, then drop the hand for the fade-out. The fermata is cut off by a vigorous preparatory beat for the following downbeat. Some other excellent examples are in the last movement of Beethoven's First Symphony. (measures 1-8 and 234-238.) Detailed conducting suggestions will be found in the *Workbook*.

The first fermata at the start of Haydn's *London* Symphony (104) is cut off by the preparatory beat to the following measure. The second fermata may be cut off completely. The cutoff might also be used to prepare for the third measure. In this case, a sharp cutoff should taper off into a soft preparation for the following piano passage.

Ex. 34

At the beginning of Schumann's First Symphony there is a fermata in the second measure, followed by an upbeat. A sharp preparation for the upbeat cuts off the fermata. In the fourth measure, another fermata is succeeded by an eighth rest. Here an especially crisp cutoff prepares for the following offbeat eighth.

At the beginning of Haydn's Symphony in E-flat Major (103) there is a fermata with a crescendo and diminuendo. This pattern has already been discussed. No further problem is involved.

Composers frequently place fermatas on rests: this should cause no difficulty. The conductor will extend such a rest to his taste. The next beat is acted out with the usual preparation. An abundance of fermatas on rests in Mozart's *Magic Flute* overture provides interesting study material (as does the first scene of this opera). Two more interesting fermatas are at the end of Cherubino's first aria in *The Marriage of Figaro* (one of them a fermata on a rest).

In the coda to the scherzo of Schumann's First Symphony there are four fermatas, two of them on rests. Schumann recognizes the problems involved in cutting off a fermata and continuing in the right time: he explicitly recommends giving two beats, although only one is needed.

A number of interesting fermatas on rests occur at the beginning of the first movement of Berlioz's *Symphonie Fantastique*. Many different kinds of fermatas may be found in the last movement of Mahler's Second Symphony (*Resurrection*). Here, as in other examples, the student will notice that fermatas on rests create the least problem.

A device occasionally found, especially in music composed since the middle of the nineteenth century, is a fermata on the barline. When the music continues up to the barline and resumes after it, this fermata requires a stop after the last beat of the preceding measure, followed by preparation for the first beat of the next measure. The procedure is quite simple:

Ex. 35

Fermatas on the barline are frequent in the symphonies of

Bruckner and Mahler. See also the scherzo of Sibelius's First Symphony.

Once in a while different instruments have fermatas on different beats within the same measure. In the second movement of César Franck's D Minor Symphony there is the following pattern:

Ex. 36

In this case one beats up to the second quarter and holds it. The fermata on the first quarter has no effect on the beat. This applies also to the first movement of the same symphony as well as to the first movement of Schumann's Fourth Symphony; the Mendelssohn overture, *Calm Sea and Prosperous Voyage*; and the introduction to Johann Strauss's waltz, *Wiener Blut*.

The following interesting example is taken from the first movement of Mahler's Ninth Symphony:

Ex. 37

There is a fermata on the third beat in the horns: first and second enter on the fourth beat and continue without any further hold. At the end of the measure, however, the cellos (and first violins) have a fermata. The horns enter after this; but if one waited until the end of the cello passage there would have to be an additional beat, making five beats in the measure. In fact, the passage has to be conducted that way. Mahler notated this passage the way he did because the uneven meter was avoided by German and Austrian romanticists (see Chapter 8).

Another interesting fermata occurs in the waltz from Strauss's *Fledermaus:*

Ex. 38

The pickup after the fermata can be done in two different ways. Either resume the eighths immediately in waltz tempo, or start them more slowly. Since waltzes are conducted one beat to the measure, the preparation, in the former case, will be on the downbeat, using it as the cutoff for the fermata. For a broader pickup, the preparation will be a second beat for a third beat in 3/4 time. The two eighths will occur on this upbeat; one beat to the measure can be resumed in the following measure.

The general pause (G. P.)

General pauses occur when the score calls for the whole orchestra to be silent for *a full measure*. Composers generally mark this measure "G. P." These G. P.'s are actually disguised fermatas, although their duration is fixed.

EXERCISE:

Ex. 39

Since the orchestra is mute during the general pause the

beat should be the "spineless" one commended when nothing "happens."

There are many general pauses (sometimes called grand pauses) in Haydn's symphonies, often not marked G. P. This is the sudden interruption in the music, so typical of Haydn's style, that creates a sensation of surprise. Mozart uses a full measure's rest in the first movement of his E-Flat Major Symphony (K.543), and two such rests in the first movement of his *Jupiter* Symphony, without marking either G. P. In the first movement of Beethoven's Fifth there are two successive measures' rest, but the pause is relatively short as there is only one beat to the measure. The same is true in the last movement of Schubert's Ninth Symphony. The first movement of Berlioz's *Symphonie Fantastique* and the scherzo in Bruckner's Seventh Symphony each have as many as three measures' rest. In Glinka's overture to *A Life for the Tsar* there is one measure's rest in slow tempo. With rests in the preceding measure, there are, altogether, seven slow beats of silence. For the beginning of a piece, this is an extremely long silence — much longer than three full measures in fast tempo.

It has been the contention of composers and writers on music — especially in our own time — that silence within a work heightens the tension and is often as important as the music itself. For this reason it may be worth while for students to study the pauses in the compositions listed below. In many instances the silence can be intensified by the conductor: by giving "spineless" beats or by keeping the baton high (as for a fermata on the barline), except that the omitted beats must be exactly in time. The orchestra should know the conductor's intention beforehand.

Examples:

BEETHOVEN: First movement of Eighth Symphony.
SCHUMANN: Scherzo and ending of First Symphony.
BRAHMS: First scherzo in Serenade, op. 11.
SCHUMANN: Second and fourth movements of Second Symphony.
WEBER: *Der Freischütz* overture (near the end).

CHOPIN: Last movement of Piano Concerto in E Minor.
BERLIOZ: Overture to *Beatrice and Benedict* (beginning).
MOUSSORGSKY: Second act of *Boris Godounov* (beginning).
MOUSSORGSKY: Scene five of *Khovantchina.*
RIMSKY-KORSAKOV: *Russian Easter* overture.
LEONCAVALLO: Prologue to *I Pagliacci.*
SIBELIUS: Last movement of First Symphony.
BERNSTEIN: Overture to *Candide.*

The caesura (*Luftpause*)

Somewhat on the same order as the fermata on a barline is the caesura (German: *Luftpause*). A caesura is indicated by ’ or // . It closely resembles the taking of breath by a singer — which is usually marked by the ’ sign — and should not be held longer than a *short* breath.

Even in instrumental music the ’ may be nothing but a breath-taking sign, not a caesura; it may occur in the winds alone with no such sign in the strings. This indicates clearly that the regular beat is to continue without interruption. Only when every instrument in the score has this mark, or when it is printed on the top (generally over the flutes as well as the first violins), does it call for a real caesura — a slight interruption of the basic tempo.

BEAT FOR A CAESURA

These small interruptions must be extremely subtle, requiring special skill. They are a problem for non-professional groups. Caesuras should be practiced extensively in class, with students singing. Start with the following simple exercise:

p *p*

Ex. 40

Preparation for the caesura is done by stopping the upbeat just before the baton reaches the top. After a small interruption flick the wrist slightly for a tiny preparation beat before the next downbeat. Some conductors give the downbeat right after the stop, with the stress on the end of this beat. For students the wrist-flick is better, but it must follow the stop quickly. The caesura will lose its meaning and sound awkward if it is more than the taking of a little breath.

Caesuras before an upbeat (or any other beat) are handled similarly. After a very brief stop the elbow might be lifted slightly to prepare for the upbeat. For any kind of caesura, however, the help of the left hand may be useful (see Chapter 6). Instead of a flick of the baton or the lifting of an elbow, a preparation beat with the left hand, at exactly the right moment, may sometimes be the best solution.

Examples:

Some caesuras have become traditional, though not marked in the score by the composer. They occur, to name a few, in the overture to Nicolai's *Merry Wives of Windsor* (above), in Weber's *Oberon* overture, and in many Strauss waltzes. For the time being, however, the student should pay attention only to the required caesuras, as found in such works as:

BEETHOVEN: Last movement of First Symphony.
SCHUMANN: Overture to *Genoveva* (just before start of allegro).
STRAUSS: *Don Juan.*
BARBER: *Adagio for Strings.*

When a caesura occurs before whole notes, as in Wagner's *Siegfried Idyll* and Moussorgsky's *Great Gate of Kiev,* the whole note is held without moving the baton, and at the end of the measure the baton is lifted for the upbeat to the next measure. Then, instead of giving a clear downbeat, the upbeat motion is continued right into the downbeat, without stopping, coming to a halt at the end of this action.

A good caesura beat demands good musicianship as well as manual dexterity. The exercise below combines many problems: fermatas, caesura, attacks on the beat and between the beats, a fade-out ending. It can be sung by three female or three male voices or a combination of both. A clear performance of this exercise indicates mastery of a number of conducting problems.

Ex. 43

Sudden change of tempo

CHANGE AFTER FERMATA OR BREAK

WHEN a new section initiates a different tempo after a fermata it is treated like the start of a piece, and the procedures described in Chapter Two apply. This kind of change occurs most frequently in first movements of classical symphonies; a slow introduction is followed by the main allegro. Many of Haydn's symphonies belong in this category. Haydn considers the allegro so independent at times that he becomes rather unorthodox. In the *Drum Roll* Symphony as well as the *Surprise*, the introductions are in slow 3/4 meter. The *Drum Roll* introduction ends with a fermata on the last full measure, whereas the *Surprise* Symphony has a quarter rest on the last beat. In both cases the following allegro starts on an upbeat: this makes for an incomplete measure in the middle of a piece, a rather unusual feature in classical music.

Ex. 44

Ex. 45

In the *Drum Roll* the fermata is cut off by a slight motion upward. This leaves the hand ready for the downbeat preparation for the following upbeat, with which to start the allegro. (The 6/8 meter is of course conducted in two beats.) In the *Surprise* Symphony, the rest on the third beat brings the hand up naturally, placing it in position for the preparation downbeat. Though the score shows no pause between introduction and allegro, the interruption caused by the preparation beat is justified because the main section starts entirely afresh. It is natural to "take a breath" before starting it. (There are similar cases in other

Haydn symphonies, among them the first movements of the *Clock* Symphony and the Symphony No. 102.)

CHANGE WITHOUT BREAK

HAYDN: Symphony No. 97 in C Major:

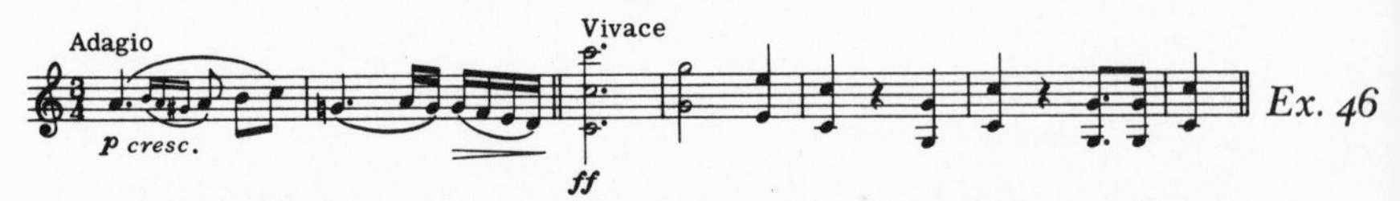

Ex. 46

In the example above the introduction moves without a break right into the vivace. The problem is not difficult because the vivace starts on a full-measure note. The second note to be played is at the beginning of the next measure, and by that time the tempo is clearly established. A strong precise beat is needed for the first note of the vivace since it starts *ff*; an upward thrust of the wrist should help. The left hand may be used as an aid.

The transition from introduction to allegro in the first movement of Beethoven's First Symphony and in Mozart's *Magic Flute* overture are other good examples (see *Workbook*).

BEETHOVEN: Second Symphony:

Ex. 47

This transition from introduction to allegro is difficult. The tempo of the allegro must be settled with the first beat, since the violins start immediately with eighth notes. What complicates matters is the fact that in the last measure of the introduction the first violins end with a sixty-fourth note run, while the rest of the strings play sixteenth note triplets simultaneously. Even without a tempo change this cross rhythm would create a problem.

It is best to anticipate the new tempo on the last beat of the introduction. A slight accelerando on the last two of the six beats is indicated. The sixty-fourth notes of the violins will then be exactly as fast as the sixteenth notes of the violas and cellos in the first allegro measure.

Anyone who objects to this procedure as not absolutely "correct" should realize that music is not mathematics and that this solution is musically more logical than the "correct" one. After all, notation has its limitations. It would have been a rather complicated matter for Beethoven to write in notes what has been suggested. He would have had to shift the allegro tempo into the last part of the previous measure.

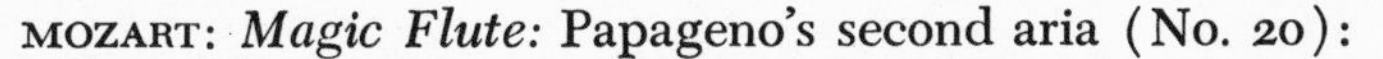
MOZART: *Magic Flute:* Papageno's second aria (No. 20):

Ex. 48

This example confirms what has been said. The first part is a 2/4 andante, ending on a fermata. After the fermata, an eighth upbeat — still in the andante section — is followed by a 6/8 pattern, marked allegro. If one conducted this passage literally, the upbeat eighth would be slower than the eighths in the following measure. Mozart, of course, did not intend this. The upbeat belongs to the new tempo. This is another example to prove that being faithful to notation may be incorrect.

In the overtures to Beethoven's *Fidelio* and Weber's *Der Freischütz,* the transition from slow tempo to fast is complicated by the fact that the fast tempo starts with a syncopated accompaniment (see Chapter Five). This added problem can be dealt with in both cases by taking the allegro exactly twice as fast as the previous slow tempo. But the orchestra must be told in advance.

ROSSINI: Overture to *William Tell:*

Ex. 49

In the last measure of the pastorale there are three triplets. On the first beat of the allegro the trumpets enter. The new tempo may be established easily because the trumpets hold the first note up to the second beat; besides, the allegro is exactly twice as fast as the previous tempo.

WAGNER: *Rienzi* Overture:

Ex. 50

Wagner asks for a sudden change to a much faster tempo

(molto più stretto). This transition will cause no trouble if the conductor knows the score thoroughly and anticipates exactly what each instrument, especially the brass, is to play in the new tempo. What is needed here is a very fast and sharp preparation for the downbeat of the stretto, followed by a clear second beat. The conductor must rely upon his ear: if the players do not follow his beat exactly he may have to catch them in the tempo in which they are playing. *Never conduct faster or slower than the musicians are actually playing.* All a conductor can do is push or hold back the orchestra with very decisive beats until it has reached the tempo he wants.

In the second movement of Beethoven's Fifth Symphony, the coda starts in faster tempo, then suddenly returns to tempo primo. This return needs clear attacks. Single instruments re-establish the tempo: if the second clarinet enters exactly on the second beat, the other woodwinds will follow.

THE LEONORE OVERTURES

Compare the transition from allegro to presto in Beethoven's second *Leonore* overture, with the similar pattern in the third. In the second the famous (and awkward) violin passage begins in the allegro tempo, climbs a step higher after every six eighths, shifts to seven eighths (an odd number which adds considerably to the rhythmic difficulty), and, at last, only one measure before the presto, has a balanced eight-note run. Then, right after this one measure, the tempo changes, creating an additional problem.

In the third *Leonore* overture the tempo change occurs earlier. After simple quarter notes in the first violins the presto sets in, coinciding with the violin run. This change should cause no difficulty since the presto starts on an eighth rest, and there is time enough to prepare it on the last quarter of the previous allegro. At the beginning of the run Beethoven uses the awkward seven-note pattern; for the following nine measures, however, he adopts a rhythmically easy eight-note run, and the entrance of the full orchestra at the climax comes with no change of tempo. Possibly Beethoven himself encountered difficulties in performance and revised the passage for the third overture. It also is more effective.

Musically another intricate change of tempo may be found toward the end of Tchaikovsky's Fifth Symphony. A majestic moderato (♩ about 80) moves into a violent presto (𝅗𝅥 144): the quarters are almost four times as fast. A very precise and incisive beat is needed for this transition.

Try the following exercises in different tempos:

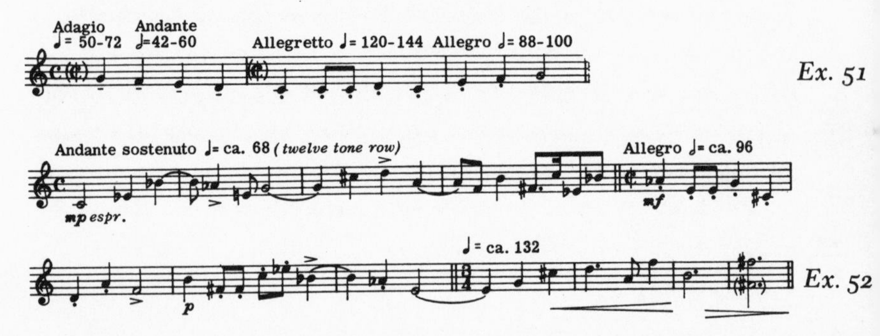

Example 52 should be played on an instrument. Singing it would at present be too difficult.

FREQUENT TEMPO CHANGES

An excellent example of frequent tempo-changes is Reinhold Glière's *Russian Sailor's Dance* from *The Red Poppy*. After the allegro introduction, the main twelve-measure theme is broad and slow. It is varied, and almost every variation has a different tempo. Each change has to be clearly indicated by a precise preparatory beat. There is danger of a poor attack when, after a fast variation, a sostenuto follows. A slight caesura is called for.

A conductor who masters his orchestra trains his group never to start any measure — after a fermata, caesura, or change of tempo — before his actual downbeat. For this purpose it is sometimes a good idea to stop unexpectedly, before giving this beat. When a player misses this stop it is an indication that the conductor has not achieved the power that compels musicians to follow him even when he does something surprising.

A number of these changes of tempo can be practiced in class, although some are strongly orchestral and do not lend themselves to singing. Members of the class might bring the instruments they are able to play. The resulting "orchestra" may be very unbalanced, with a bassoon playing a cello part or vice versa, and a clarinet playing violin or viola parts. There may also be students able to fill in missing instruments at the piano. This conglomeration will not sound like an orchestra, but it can serve the purpose to determine the effectiveness of the student conductor's beat. The only concern is the student's ability to convey his rhythmic and dynamic conception to his players; furthermore, he will experience a new sensation, that of conducting instruments instead of voices. Some examples in Chapter Two and Three could now be repeated with "orchestra."

Examples:

BEETHOVEN: Scherzo of Seventh Symphony.
BEETHOVEN: Third and fourth movements of Ninth Symphony.
BEETHOVEN: Finale of *Eroica* Symphony.
WEBER: Overture to *Oberon.*
ROSSINI: Overture to *William Tell.*
MENDELSSOHN: Finale of *Reformation* Symphony.
BRAHMS: Finale of Fourth Symphony.
WAGNER: Prelude to *Die Meistersinger.*
FRANCK: Symphony in D Minor (seven changes in first movement).
WAGNER: Overture to *The Flying Dutchman.*
MASCAGNI: Introduction to *Cavalleria Rusticana.*
TCHAIKOVSKY: Scherzo of Fourth Symphony.

The second movement of Tchaikovsky's Fifth Symphony contains an interesting example. Here the tempo changes from allegro to andante cantabile. At the same time the meter changes from 4/4 to 12/8. As the 𝅗𝅥 of the allegro equals a ♩. in the new tempo, the pizzicato chords will be spaced identically to the full orchestra chords in the previous allegro. Consequently the change here is really one of meter, not of tempo. The student will find additional tempo changes in this symphony.

Change of meter

Change of meter usually, but not always, coincides with change of tempo. Quite often the new meter does not require any change of beat at all. A few examples will illustrate.

> BEETHOVEN: Scherzo of Eroica Symphony: Change from 3/4 to ₵ and back; conductor continues beating each measure with single beats.
> LISZT: *Faust* Symphony: Meter shifts frequently in first allegro (4/4 – 3/4 – 2/4).
> BRAHMS: First movement of Third Symphony: Meter shifts between 6/4 and 9/4 (two and three beats).
> BRAHMS: Third movement of Second Symphony: Meter changes from 3/4 to 2/4; two quarters of new meter (a full measure) equal one quarter of previous meter.

In the Coronation Scene in Moussogorsky's *Boris Godounov* the meter alternates frequently between 3/4 and 2/4 time. Similar shifts may be found in other parts of this opera. (Changes of meter are especially frequent in Slavic music – see Chapter Eight.)

In the second scene of the last act of Wagner's *Tristan and Isolde* 3/4 and 4/4 meters take turns. Later on even 5/4 meter appears, until then practically unknown in German music (see Chapter Eight). Tristan's frenzy could have no better expression than this strange meter.

The trio in the scherzo of Borodin's First Symphony starts with the following melody:

Ex. 5

It does not lose its character by constant repetition and may well be done in different tempos, and legato as well as staccato.

In Puccini's *Il Tabarro* (introduction) the meter shifts continually between 12/8, 6/8, and 9/8 meter.

In the overture to *Candide* Bernstein constantly alternates between two alla breve measures and one measure in 3/2 time. He starts this pattern in connection with the most expressive melodic passage in the work.

When Offenbach returns to the initial theme in his overture to *La belle Hélène,* he moves from a lilting 6/4 waltz-like section to a sharp 2/4 march tempo. This does not happen suddenly; there are, first, two measures of the march tempo, followed by a return to the 6/4 meter. On the third and fourth repetitions only half the 6/4 meter recurs; thereafter the march takes over entirely. This sounds more complicated than it actually is; the beat remains the same. One measure of the 2/4 time equals one beat of the 6/4 meter or a full measure of the 3/4 meter. The only difference is that the conductor must give two beats for the 2/4 meter, to achieve a sharper march rhythm. The conductor who has become used to giving subdivisions, and has trained his orchestra accordingly, should have no difficulty conducting this passage.

In music by Debussy, Mahler, Richard Strauss – and especially Bartok, Stravinsky, and most contemporary composers – meter changes recur so often that the conductor must be thoroughly acquainted with the score. Otherwise he may become confused, with resultant chaos in the orchestra.

Constant meter changes within one piece are characteristic of a special kind of Spanish and Latin American music. This dance rhythm alternates between 3/4 and 6/8 meter. The eighths remain the same throughout.* Each meter is treated exactly according to its rule of accentuation – that is, the 3/4 meter has a beat

* By mistake this meter change may be conducted 3/4 ♩ ♩ ♩ ‖ 6/8 ♪♪♪ ♪♪♪. In this case the quarters remain the same, not the eighths. This is, of course, wrong, unless marked by the composer ♩ = ♩. . Some editions reverse this marking and print ♩. = ♩ . They contend that the ♩. of the new meter equals a ♩ of the old. The other marking denotes that what had been a ♩ is now a ♩. . Both versions may be found; the meaning in each case should be self-explanatory.

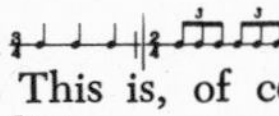

on each quarter while the 6/8 has its usual emphasis on the first and fourth eighth. Consequently, it will be conducted: $\frac{3}{4}$ | $\frac{6}{8}$ and should be practiced in class with one student conducting and the others clapping, first all eighths, but with the right accentuation, then the quarters and dotted quarters alternatively. It is a very useful exercise.

Gradual change of tempo

Like the gradual crescendo and diminuendo, the gradual change of tempo was not known in the music of the baroque period. Still, Bach and Handel did not desire their music played in a metronomically rigid tempo, even if the changes were not indicated. The same is true of Mozart and Haydn. Mozart's music, especially his operatic work, requires slight tempo fluctuation though he does not mark it. Haydn did use a few ritardandos in his later works (written after Mozart's death), but it was Beethoven who introduced both ritardando and stringendo (accelerando) signs, especially in his later works.

The coda in the finale of Beethoven's Fifth Symphony contains a speed-up, marked *sempre più allegro*. The increase in speed leads from the alla breve beat of the allegro to the single beat of the presto. The tempo change will cause no difficulty so long as the conductor does not start accelerating before the measure in which Beethoven marked it. There is a tendency among young conductors to begin speeding up two measures earlier: no doubt there is a certain urgency and tension in these measures; but it is a misconception to believe that *any* growing tension must be accompanied by an accelerando (see Chapter 18). Beethoven knew exactly what he was doing, indicating the *più alle*gro where he did: during the following measures only quarter notes are used, not eighths as before, where an accelerando could easily cause the orchestra to fall apart. Pushing the tempo should be no problem.

ACCELERANDO

The feeling the conductor should have, when accelerating the orchestra, is like "pushing" or "egging on." Strong, sharp, and precise beats are necessary, with short motions. The players will follow him if his beat cuts through. Sometimes, in trying to speed up, student conductors feel the weight of the orchestra on their arms; as a result their beat becomes ponderous. Players react to this heaviness and are apt to play with more emphasis instead of more speed. They may even slow down. The beat, therefore, must be short and whip-like.

Additional Beethoven examples are the scherzo of the Pastoral Symphony (*sempre più stretto*); the scherzo of the Ninth Symphony (*stringendo il tempo*); and the end of the finale of the Ninth Symphony (*stringendo il tempo, sempre più allegro*).

RITARDANDO

Slowing down causes less difficulty: the conductor simply broadens his beat. Once in a while, however, a ritardando may require a change in the beat-pattern. In the scherzo of Beethoven's Fifth Symphony, for example, conducted one beat to the measure, the ritardando in the seventh measure may best be accomplished by giving three beats.

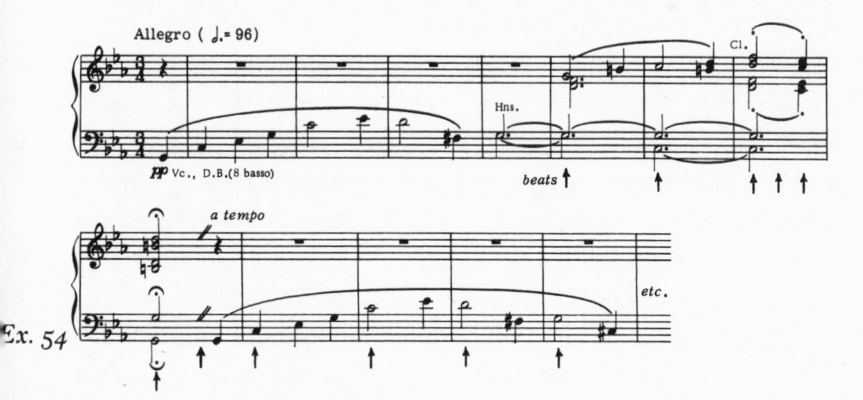

Ex. 54

The tempo change should never be sudden. When the beat-pattern is changed during a ritardando – as in this example from a single beat to three – the change must be extremely clear. In the first measure the one-beat pattern should be kept, while attaching to this one beat the two- and three- of the three-beat pattern in a "spineless" way. In the next measure (which should be slower) three clear beats should be given.

As in an accelerando, if the passage occurs on a succession of fast notes, a ritardando may cause rhythmic unevenness. In the aria *Celeste Aida*, from Verdi's *Aida*, it is dangerous to change the tempo after the fermata (*un trono vicino al sol*), as some conductors do. In Dvořáks third *Legend* a ritardando coincides with sudden triplets – up to this point eighths are played – and this passage requires a clear beat and careful rehearsing.

RETURN TO TEMPO

In many Strauss waltzes the motion is interrupted by a fermata, and then the tempo is gradually picked up. The conductor should start, after the hold, with three beats to a measure, speed

Ex. 55

up, and after a few measures reach the one-beat waltz tempo again.

The occurrence of gradual tempo changes increased during the development of romanticism. While Mendelssohn, a "classic" romanticist, seldom asks for them, Schumann, who is more emotional, speeds up the tempo gradually from the slow introduction to the main allegro in three of his four symphonies and the *Manfred* overture. Striking examples of the speed-ups may be found in the finale of Brahms's First Symphony; these are some of the most rhapsodic passages in symphonic literature. A composer of such highly emotional disposition as Tchaikovsky makes frequent use of both gradual retarding and speed-ups. A notable illustration of this occurs in the finale of his *Symphonie Pathétique.* Bruckner's and Mahler's symphonies provide a wide range of gradual tempo changes, as do the works of Strauss and – in a more subtle way – Debussy.

With the more formalistic approach of contemporary composers, modern scores, though complex in harmony and meter, show few accelerando and ritardando markings. Stravinsky's earlier works (especially *Petroushka*) contain them, but from his middle period on, although there are many tempo and meter changes, there are few gradual ones. This is characteristic of neoclassical music.

To obtain the feel of the beat during tempo changes, exercises, introducing both accelerando and ritardando at unexpected moments in well-known songs, should be very helpful. It should be clearly understood that these tempo changes need not be musically justified; on the contrary, they should come as surprises and also include changes of beat-patterns from one beat to three beats, two beats to four, and vice versa (sub-divisions).

5 Accents

Accents, syncopation

Accents

JUST as a vigorous beat should be given for forte passages and a gentle one for dolce and grazioso sections, so a sharp beat should help in the execution of accents. The same applies to syncopations, which suggest accenting an offbeat note, and are frequently stressed by added accents. Especially sharp motions are necessary when conducting non-professionals.

It is important to realize that accents need a preparatory beat. The orchestra must be alerted *before* the accented notes occur. It is too late to conduct them on the beat on which they should be executed.

There are three methods of preparation:

1] Emphasize the beat before the accent. This is done with an arm movement more sweeping than usual, without changing the tempo.

2] Move the elbow slightly upward, between preparatory and accent beat.

3] Help with the left hand (see Chapter Six).

Accents are marked either > or ∧. *Sf* or *sfz* (sforzando) and *fz* (forzato) are also used. *Rinf.* or *rfz* (rinforzando) indicate an emphasis on a short phrase, not one note; *fp* (fortepiano) is not just an accent – it indicates that after the accent the tone immediately turns soft (see Chapters 17 and 19).

There is quite a difference between the strong vigorous accents in Beethoven's work and the softer, more subtle ones in Mozart and Schubert. Naturally, sharp accents must be stressed with a strong, more obvious beat. For softer ones the beat may be confined to an almost unnoticeable move of the elbow, or a very slight assistance by the left hand. The student will choose the motion that fits his style. As in all conducting, any awkwardness must be avoided. Some conductors get good results with nothing more than a barely emphasized preparatory beat.

EXAMPLES

A few examples follow from classical and romantic music.

There are, of course, accents in most works in musical literature; this selection is intended to show typical examples.

Mozart, even when he wrote *fp* in a piano passage, wanted only a slight accent, not an actual forte-piano. In the development of the first movement of his *Haffner* Symphony (K. 385), and in the introduction to his *Prague* Symphony (K. 504), the *fp*'s represent no more than sighs. Any sharpness must be avoided. In the minuet of his E-flat Major (K. 543), and in the second theme of the finale of his G Minor Symphony (K. 550), he was even cautious enough to mark these accents *mfp*.

In the bass part of the retransition in the first movement of the G Minor Symphony (K. 550), and at the end of the finale of the *Jupiter* (K. 551), the accents should be sharper (forte) but never overstressed.

When Haydn wants slight accents he generally marks them >, as in the introduction and second movement of his *Drum Roll* Symphony (103), and in the introduction to his *Military* Symphony. In the latter introduction he applies the *sf* sign for loud accents.

In the finales of his *Clock* and *Surprise* symphonies, there are strongly accented downbeats. Haydn's music is earthier than Mozart's, and the accents should be more vigorous.

Beethoven's music is so rich in accents – and generally rather sharp ones – that hundreds could be mentioned. Below are a few unusual ones.

Although the main theme of his Second Symphony has a certain lightness at first, he uses sharp-edged, almost harsh accents in its development.

In the forte variation in the *Eroica* finale, the theme is strongly accented in the bass; and the last climax of this symphony is reached with sharply lashing strokes, all accented.

The third theme in the last movement of the Fifth has *fp* marks every two measures (later, when this theme is played forte, they become *sf*'s). The very last presto, using the same theme, also has *fp* marks. Because of the climactic drive of this section, the piano is often neglected. It is very important.

Accents in Schubert's music have a subtlety similar to Mozart. Although there are some strongly accented climaxes in the dramatic parts of his last two symphonies, it is worth studying the minute stresses in the soft sections, especially in the *Unfinished.* The accents in the *Rosamunde* ballet music should also be done with delicacy. To neglect them (as is often the case) deprives this work of its Viennese charm.

The *idée fixe* of Berlioz's *Symphonie Fantastique* is marked with many accents, slight and sharp. The excitement and spasmodic heartbeat of the ardent lover are characterized by these fluctuations.

Schumann loves accents. Sometimes they can be found on every beat. Especially worth studying are the main themes of the first movements and scherzos of his First and Fourth Symphonies.

Though Brahms's symphonies have even more contrasting orchestral shades than Schumann's, he did not use accents so often as his older friend. There are, however, many of them in the last movement of his First Symphony.

Syncopation

One of the oldest and most basic syncopated patterns is:  . It was originally used for accompanying voices, as in the aria *Divinités du Styx* from Gluck's *Alceste,* and and in the *Melancholic* from Dittersdorf's *Tournament of Temperaments.* Romantic composers often shifted this pattern to the themes themselves, where it became a mainstay of highly emotional melodic expression. We find it in Berlioz's *Symphonie Fantastique,* in Schumann's Second Symphony (adagio), and in Verdi's operas, especially *Aida* (Act IV). Brahms was particularly fond of this pattern (in melody and accompaniment) and it may be found in most movements of his symphonies. In his Second Symphony he elaborates on it:  .

It becomes still more complex in the first movement of Tchaikovsky's *Pathétique*:  .

At the start of his tone poem, *Death and Transfiguration,*

Strauss uses the same pattern but with triplets and eighths reversed. (It is also worth while to examine the beginning of Act II of Wagner's *Götterdämmerung.*)

OFFBEAT ACCENTS

The accenting of one (or two) offbeats in a measure is probably the most regular kind of syncopation. This syncopation is, for instance, typical for the Polish dance, the Mazurka. These offbeat notes may occur within a melodic line or even stand by themselves. They are found very often in recitatives, when the orchestra enters on offbeat notes and at times even between beats. For practice purposes try the following exercise:

Ex. 56

f

In Mozart accented syncopation should be performed as subtly as any other kind of accent. Some examples are the allegro in the *Magic Flute* overture, the minuet in the *Haffner* Symphony (K. 385), and the seventh measure of the andante in the G Minor Symphony (K. 550).

Haydn loves these little rhythmical extravagances. Examine the main theme of the first movement in the *Drum Roll* Symphony (103): in this 6/8 meter the stress is on the third and sixth eighth. Also note the concluding theme of the exposition in the *London* (104), and the E-flat Major Symphony (99), as well as the minuet in the *London* Symphony.

Beethoven makes ample use of syncopation to heighten the dramatic expressiveness of his musical ideas, beginning with his First Symphony. The syncopations at the end of his Second Symphony show progress in impact and vigor.

The Eroica represents a vast step in the new direction. The first movement is full of offbeat rhythms. Second-beat accents are frequent, as they are both here and in the Fourth Symphony. At the very end of the *Eroica* the violins perform offbeat chords that need special attention. (The same kind of offbeat chords are played by violins in the famous cancan in Offenbach's *Orpheus in the Underworld*, but very much faster.)

In the Eighth Symphony it is interesting to note that the first theme of the first movement has strong offbeat accents in the development, whereas it has no accents at all in its first version.

The *Coriolanus* overture furnishes an excellent model for rhythm-study. After the introductory thrusts, the main theme starts softly and in a few measures builds up a dramatic climax ending on the fourth quarter of the sixth measure (offbeat and between beats because the overture is conducted with two beats to a measure). Then Beethoven repeats the procedure (one tone lower), and again reaches the climax in the sixth measure, but this time on the second quarter. Syncopations can be found throughout the overture. A rather intricate pattern is the following: . The higher voices perform the top rhythm and the lower voices the bottom pattern. If done accurately, the eighths should follow each other so evenly that the rhythmic pattern will sound: . This pattern may be used as a class exercise, with some students clapping the top passage and some the bottom. Students might again take turns conducting.

A rather odd syncopated section occurs in Beethoven's third Leonore overture. A chromatic scale is started in the upper strings. The lower strings take part in the same scale, but always one quarter behind the violins. It sounds as if the basses are unable to keep up, and actually they do not catch up before the resolving climax, coinciding with the recapitulation. The interval clashes — major sevenths throughout, creating rather harsh sounds — are not relieved until three measures before the resolution, when they turn into a dominant seventh chord and, though still syncopated, are thus within the same harmony.

A great many syncopations appear in the works of Schumann and especially Brahms. Here are some examples:

The main theme of the first movement of Schumann's Second Symphony is accented throughout on the second beat. The conductor must avoid overemphasizing this syncopation, or the movement may become rather tedious. Schumann himself must have felt this danger, because he sometimes shifts the accent to the third beat.

In the scherzo in Schumann's Fourth Symphony (conducted with one beat to a measure), there is an accent on every second beat between measures nine and fourteen.

In the finale of Brahms's First Symphony the following rather awkward pattern is carried for quite a while: . The rests on the first and third beats (in allegro tempo) occur in all voices of the orchestra.

In the finale of the Second Symphony the first forte entrance by the full orchestra happens after an eighth's rest in all voices. Later Brahms accents a great deal on the second quarter in each measure.

TWO-BEAT RHYTHM IN 3/4 TIME

A syncopation that may create problems and that occurs quite frequently is a two-beat rhythm in triple meter. It can be found as early as the minuet in Mozart's G Minor Symphony (K. 550).

Allegretto

Ex. 57

f

Beethoven applies this pattern again and again in the first movement of the *Eroica*, and it furnishes the basic rhythm of the scherzo in his Fourth Symphony.

There is a classic example of this rhythm in the last movement of Schumann's Piano Concerto.

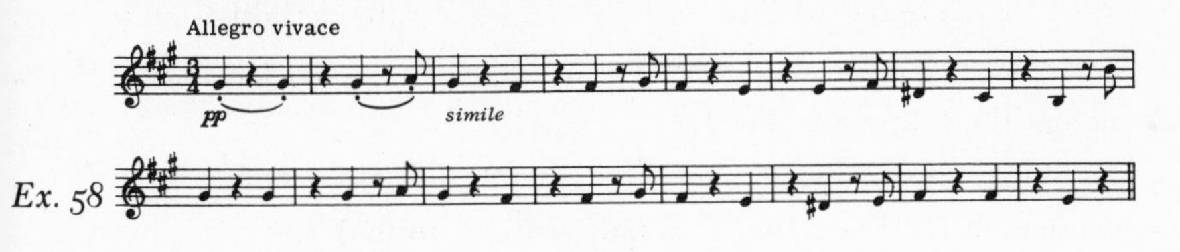

In this passage the triple beat is practically eliminated; the second measure starts with a rest in all instruments. The fact that this movement is conducted with one beat to the measure complicates matters. The young conductor must feel the rhythm, and not be confused by the syncopation.

This is a preliminary exercise: . This exercise should be practiced by singing the syncopated rhythm on one note and beating the triple meter with a single downbeat for each measure; or by beating the syncopation with one hand and the meter with the other. When the student feels sure of this rhythm he might conduct it with the class clapping and then singing, or playing the Schumann example.

Another good example for study is the following passage from the second movement of Tchaikovsky's Fifth Symphony:

Ex. 59

This excerpt should be conducted in four beats to the measure. Again, a student should conduct it with the remainder of the class either singing or playing it. This passage causes added difficulty because there is a directive to retard the orchestra slightly before the following climax.

When the tempo is slow enough for the triple meter to be conducted in three, the syncopation is no problem. Even when conducted in one, matters will become simpler if the orchestra plays, not rests, on the second downbeat (contrary to the Schumann example). This is the case in the waltz from Tchaikovsky's *Sleeping Beauty*, which has the same syncopation. The normal waltz beat, however, continues in the accompaniment.

Additional examples are the first movement of Schumann's *Rhenish* (Third) Symphony, the first movement of Brahms's Third Symphony (in 6/4 meter), and parts of the finale of Berlioz's *Symphonie Fantastique* (in 6/8).

Another interesting syncopation problem presents itself at the start of Schumann's *Manfred* overture. This work opens with syncopations:

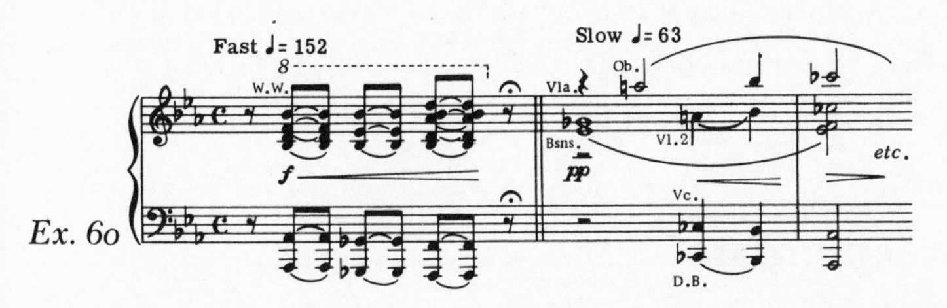

Ex. 60

A very sharp preparation on the downbeat should effect a clear entrance of the orchestra; the second beat should determine the exact tempo. Here we have another case in which it might be advisable to draw the baton back before the first (preparation) downbeat, precisely a full beat ahead.

Additional examples:

SMETANA: Overture to *The Bartered Bride.*
BORODIN: Polovetsian Dances from *Prince Igor* (many examples).
STRAVINSKY: *Rite of Spring* (abounds in complicated syncopations).
WAGNER: End of Act I of *Die Meistersinger.*
PUCCINI: Introduction to *Tosca.*
COPELAND: *Outdoor* overture.

The following exercise combines fermatas, accents, syncopation, and dynamics:

EXAMPLE

LATIN AMERICAN RHYTHMS

There is a good deal of shifting of accents in Latin American music; the characteristic change of meter has already been discussed. The rhumba has the following pattern: ♩. ♪ ♩ ♩ Conduct four beats to a measure and accent the second beat as a preparation for the offbeat. A slight lifting of the elbow will generally bring about the desired effect. These accentuations should be very subtle: the student will find himself doing it naturally when he has absorbed the rhythm. Parts of Gershwin's *Rhapsody in Blue* use this rhythm.

CROSS RHYTHM

This occurs when one voice has eighths while another has triplets. Actually, any combination of two different metric patterns belongs to this category, such as four against three, five against four, and so forth. Cross rhythm may be found as early as the eighteenth century (in Haydn and Mozart, especially in Mozart's operas). Performance creates no problems. In general, a melody using eighths is based on a triplet accompaniment.

In the introduction to Beethoven's Second Symphony there are sixteenths and sixteenths triplets. This is similar to eighths and triplets. One voice, however, is not a mere accompaniment to the other: each moves independently. Beethoven makes frequent use of cross rhythm.

EXAMPLES:

Funeral March in *Eroica* Symphony.
Finale of *Eroica* Symphony.
Second movement of Fourth Symphony.
Second Movement of Fifth Symphony.

The last movement listed also contains the following pattern (which is already to be found in the second movement of the First Symphony): .

Schubert uses it in the ballet music to *Rosamunde*, and in the first and last movements of his Ninth Symphony.

The student conductor will notice that these cross rhythms are often more complex in slow movements than in fast, and that difficulties increase when the even flow of either triplets or eighths is interrupted. Syncopations in one voice may add another problem. Brahms especially favors these devices; there are few movements in any of his works without cross rhythms, often intricate ones.

The three-against-two design is actually nothing but a two-beats in triple-meter pattern. The exercise recommended on page 64 should be extended to four-against-three, five-against-four, and even five-against-three. A prospective conductor will find it valuable to be familiar with rhythmically conflicting patterns.

Sometimes two meters are indicated at the same time, as in the quintet from Bizet's *Carmen*. Here we encounter 2/8 meter (with 4/16) together with 6/16.

When the conductor has to beat a meter different from the one actually being played these cross rhythms create an additional problem. If he himself is absolutely sure of the rhythm he should have no difficulty. Of course, inexperienced players may easily get mixed up. The ideal solution appears when the conductor is capable of conducting one meter with one hand and the other with the other hand. One further example is the end of the aria, *Ritorna Vincitor*, from Verdi's *Aida* (four-against-six).

A passage from Berlioz's *King Lear* overture has the following pattern:

Ex. 62

This excerpt may well be used as an exercise.

The chimes at the end of Mahler's Second Symphony introduce the following pattern:

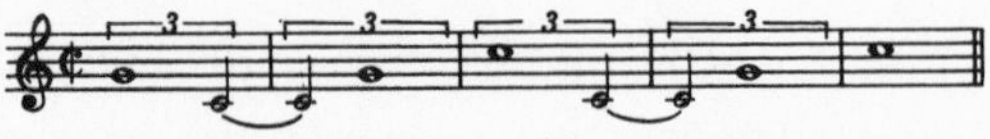

Ex. 63

This pattern is even more difficult to perform correctly and should also be used as an exercise.

Not a cross rhythm but one of the most striking early examples of combined meters takes place in Mozart's *Don Giovanni.* In the second act, three orchestras play on stage for the entertainment of the Don's guests. This is the pattern:

Ex. 64

The conductor should beat the 3/4 meter; this orchestra is the largest one and the singers also have 3/4 meter. The other two groups should have leaders capable of picking up the right time from the conductor's beat.

In the following pattern, occurring in Hindemith's second *Kammermusik* (piano concerto), the beat of the conductor can help only one group (unless he is able to conduct both meters simultaneously – see Chapter 6):

Ex. 65

After three measures of 4/4 meter and eight measures of 3/8 meter the two groups meet for the first time on a common downbeat. (This is an exceptional problem, and not to be solved by beginners.)

Music has become so complex in the twentieth century that unusual cross rhythms have to be expected. In general they are confined to cross rhythms within the same meter or even within the same beat. The student should find it worth while to study modern scores from this point of view, and to discuss conducting methods (Mahler's *Song of the Earth* is recommended, among others).

In baroque music cross rhythms were practically unknown. A rare example is Bach's Triple Concerto in A Minor, where sometimes two notes are set against three. Later in the same piece it does seem as if Bach is setting three notes against four, but in baroque time this was not done. The pattern occurring together with should be played .

Practice and study of this chapter should be continued during work on the following chapters. Example 66 may be used as an additional exercise.

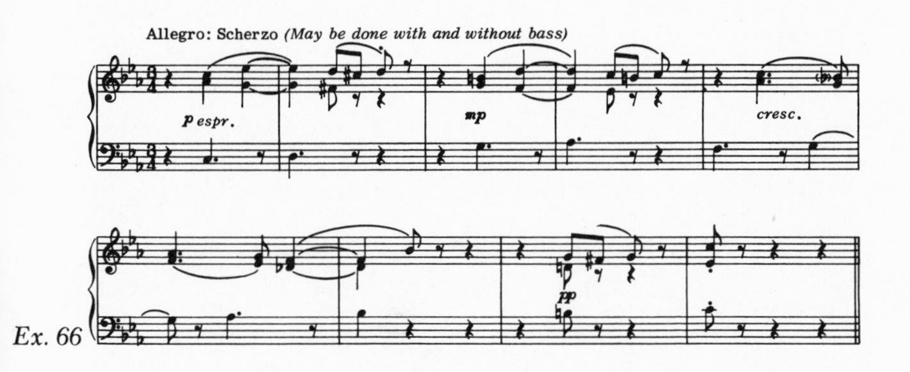

Ex. 66

6 *The left hand*

IT HAS occasionally been suggested that the student employ the left hand for assistance with the more complex beats. For elementary exercises the left hand has been excluded; beating the basic patterns constantly with both hands is a rather ordinary and often amateurish way of conducting, and can become a bad habit. When the student has become accustomed to using the right hand alone for the beat, however, he should gradually avail himself of the valuable services of the left.

DYNAMICS

One of the main duties of the left hand is to regulate dynamics. A sudden warning signal – the outstretched hand, palm directed toward the instruments to be hushed – should be capable of softening these voices. If this is not sufficient an added sideward shaking of the hand, as if trying to eradicate the sound, should be helpful. As in so many cases, the exact manner of gesturing depends upon the conductor. The student should discover for himself which way feels most natural. He should watch good professional conductors: some achieve the softening effect in manners different from the ones mentioned here. Some conductors place a finger – or even the whole hand – in front of their mouths; others hunch their shoulders as if about to crouch; some even bend their knees to make themselves smaller, thus trying to induce the orchestra to play softly, but this is generally an unesthetic sight. (Beethoven is said to have used this method, and to have appeared rather grotesque doing it.) The left hand can do the job very well while the right hand should continue, undisturbed, with the regular beat. The motions of both hands should become entirely independent of each other.

Although experience shows that a conductor will use his left hand chiefly for softening, he may also use it for increasing power by "drawing out" the tone. A gradual crescendo may be helped by slowly raising the left hand, palm upward; the climax is reached when the hand is highest. A gradual and extended diminuendo may be aided by lowering the left hand slowly, palm downward. When an extremely fine and sensitive tone is desired, pinch thumb and index finger together while stretching the other fingers — as if one were talking about something extremely delicate.

After it has become habitual to beat the standard patterns with the right hand alone, the student may at times find it helpful to beat with both hands. He may feel he can thus achieve greater precision; in strongly rhythmic passages and climaxes it may add to the suggestive strength of the beat. For highly emotional, sweeping effects, it may even be more effective to move both hands in parallel — instead of the usual contrary — motion. (This device should be applied on rare occasions.) However, the use of the left hand for duplicating the beat will lose all its impact if the conductor employs it constantly. When saved for special occasions, it will produce the desired effect.

The left hand may also be very valuable for showing strings the way to bow. Long, sweeping motions — from front to back for the downbows and from back to front for the upbows — will induce the players to use full length legato bowings. (This applies only to the players on the left side and possibly in front of the conductor.) Short, forceful punches will indicate a martellato.

Some conductors shake their hands in a way that imitates a vibrato. Beginners should avoid such motions because they may appear awkward. After some experience a conductor will use adequate gestures naturally. All the motions a conductor makes should look esthetically appealing. The left hand should always be used with fingers held together, not spread. Here, too, the student should observe his actions in front of a mirror.

HELD NOTES

The left hand has been mentioned previously (see Chapter 3) for giving a beat while the right hand is holding a fermata. A kind of reverse action is advisable when one group is required to hold a note through a full measure. Often, when the right hand gives the upbeat for the following measure, musicians holding the note stop it right there, not continuing it to the next downbeat. If the left hand remains high during this upbeat, and descends together with the right hand on the following downbeat, it will induce the group to hold the note as long as required.

Often the wind section holds notes for a number of measures. Here again the left hand, kept high, will induce the players to hold the note relentlessly and to stop it only when the hand moves down.

A similar procedure is useful for conducting an unusual passage in Mendelssohn's *Ruy Blas* overture. In the introduction slow chords in the winds are followed by an allegro molto in the strings. This pattern occurs three times; the third time, however, the allegro is not yet completed when the lento starts:

Ex. 67

On the lento the right hand gives the forte strongly accented, and holds the note as long as needed. The left hand marks the two light pizzicatos in the strings in the allegro tempo.

The left hand may also be assigned the task of waving off a premature or incorrect attack by an instrument. If such a mishap should occur during a performance, the conductor should, of course, avoid making an obvious gesture. The motion with the left hand can be made close to and in front of the body.

SYNCOPATIONS

The left hand can be very helpful in giving beats independent of the right hand beats. It can, for instance, indicate syncopations (see Chapter 5).

A more complex use is the handling of three beats in 4/4 meter: . The student will need much experience before he can master this. As a preliminary exercise, he might try beating two beats with one hand, against three with the other; then try three against four (see Chapter 5).

Ex. 68

The student should not become discouraged if he has difficulty beating with both hands independently. The right hand *always* (even in the second measure) beats the basic meter. This example is useful as a class exercise only if the three notes in the triplets each have exactly the same duration.

Fortunately, this kind of syncopation, or rather cross rhythm, occurs rarely. When it does occur, as in Berlioz's *King Lear* overture and in the last movement of Mahler's Second Symphony (see Chapter 5), a fairly competent orchestra should be able to play the triplets despite the two or four beats of the conductor. But this will only be the case if the conductor himself has a clear conception of the rhythm.

The use of the left hand for cuing purposes is dealt with in the following chapter. Some conductors cue by pointing very obviously to players with their index fingers, but this method is not advisable as a habit.

The left hand can be of assistance during sudden tempo changes. It can give the preparatory beat in the new tempo while the right hand finishes the measure in the previous tempo.

From this point on sudden tempo changes should cause less difficulty if assisted by the left hand.

Tempo changes discussed in Chapter 4 should now be tackled again, this time with the help of the left hand. The student might also conduct music with marked diminuendos and crescendos, or even without such markings, and achieve these dynamic changes by use of the left hand. Exercises for beating fermatas and caesuras should also be repeated.

7 Cuing

SOME renowned conductors of excellently trained orchestras do not give any cues at all. They feel that the main job of the conductor is spiritual and that during a concert all technical guidance should be reduced to a minimum. On the other hand, there are conductors of professional orchestras who – especially when conducting from memory – cue constantly and conspicuously. This is not only unnecessary but at times may be more distracting than helpful, even if listeners are impressed with the conductor's knowledge of the score.

The situation is different when it comes to non-professional orchestras. The players generally have had ample rehearsal time and should be familiar with their entrances, but lack of experience causes insecurity. Cues should be handled clearly but not obviously; in general, directing the beat toward the player will suffice. The use of the left hand may be advantageous, especially if the player sits on the left side of the conductor – but large, extravagant gestures should be avoided. In many cases the eyes alone may be sufficient.

For an important entrance of an instrument or group, a quick, encouraging glance toward the player one or two measures before the actual cue – depending upon the tempo of the piece – may be very helpful; but the motions of the hand must not interfere, and this preparing glimpse must never be mistaken for the actual cue. It should express nothing more than the notice or warning: "Be ready."

When an instrument has had many measures of rest it is often necessary to provide a cue for a very insignificant entrance. These secondary attacks need special attention, as they are more apt to be missed than important solos.

A cue should be treated somewhat like the start of a piece: a preparation is needed. Giving the cue *on* the beat on which the instrument enters would be too late.

CUING EXERCISES

At this stage of his studies the student should give as many cues as he can master. It is important that he shows that he

7
Cuing

knows every detail of the score. At home and in class, while conducting to a recording, the student should imagine an orchestra in front of him and signal the cues in the exact direction of each imaginary instrument. (It has been said in the Introduction and in Chapter 1 that this is, of course, not *conducting* but being conducted *by* the recording; records should be used only for a check-up on knowledge of the score and, especially, the cues.) It is important that the seating of this "orchestra" be identical to the seating of an actual orchestra—preferably one in which members of the class themselves participate. The seating of such an orchestra has presumably been established with acoustics in mind and therefore will be more or less permanent.

An experienced conductor knows that the seating of an orchestra varies with the stage and hall (see Chapter 23), and that if he is to conduct another group he must familiarize himself with the different set-up. Even cuing becomes a habit and, with growing experience, is done almost instinctively. For that reason, before starting a rehearsal, a guest conductor will usually take a few minutes' time to be quite sure where every instrument is placed. If the seating differs greatly from the one he is accustomed to, he is likely to find it difficult for a while to give all cues in the right direction.

There are schools of conducting that make cuing a student's principal task. It is not. Eventually a conductor who masters the score will provide the necessary cues quite automatically.

The following exercise should be practiced for cuing purposes. It is obvious that both hands must act independently. The right hand has stressed and unstressed beats, whereas the left hand must give sharp and soft cues. The exercise may be done vocally or instrumentally:

Ex. 69

Again, different tempos should be used. Dynamics may be changed.

8 Unusual and combined metrical patterns

METERS such as 5/4 and 7/4 have not been dealt with previously because they are most unusual. School orchestra conductors may never come across them at all. This book, however, would not be complete without dealing with them, since it aims to furnish the student with tools to handle any type of rhythm or meter problem.

Uneven meters may be found in Eastern music (especially Russian) dating from the early romantic period. They have not been accepted in Western music until this century, however, and recent acceptance is due chiefly to Eastern influence.

5/4 METER

One of the most popular pieces in 5/4 meter is the second movement of Tchaikovsky's *Symphonie Pathétique* (No. 6). In contemporary music there is sometimes a 5/4 meter without any noticeable rhythmic subdivision within the bar, but generally it is a combination of 2/4 and 3/4 meter. In the Tchaikovsky example there clearly are two plus three beats. The pattern, derived from a combination of the 4/4 and 6/8 beat, is shown in Fig. 22.

Fig. 22

Sixty years before Tchaikovsky composed his Sixth Symphony, Michael Glinka wrote *A Life for the Tsar,* an opera significant in music history as one of the first masterworks to connect Western and Russian musical development. The following song, in 5/4 meter, is a choral piece from this opera:

Ex. 70

Fig. 23

For use as an exercise this example may be transposed a fourth down (G Major). In contrast to the Tchaikovsky it has the second accent on the fourth beat, not the third. This secondary accent is much less pronounced, however, than in Tchaikovsky's piece. The conducting pattern is Fig. 23.

In measures six and eight, this Glinka song has the second accent on the third beat, as in the Tchaikovsky example. For these measures, therefore, the first pattern should be used.

COMBINED METERS

An interesting example of meter combination is Feodor's song, in Moussorgsky's *Boris Godounov:*

Ex. 71

The 5/4 meter is clearly three plus two.

The example below can serve as a class exercise in sight-reading and conducting — as well as ear training, if some singers sing incorrect notes with which to test the conductor. The conducting of unusual meters is at this point most important.

Ex. 72

In addition to 5/4 and 7/4, 5/8 and 7/8 meters will be found. The tempo of all these meters will often be too fast to be beaten in single quarters or eighths. When the articulation is two plus three and four plus three, two quarters or eighths need only a single beat; the last quarter or eighth should be indicated by a slight flick of the wrist upward, before the following downbeat. The last three eighths (or quarters) may as an alternative be done on a single beat: consequently, there will be only two (or three) beats, with the last one slightly longer than the first one (or two). When it is three plus two (in 5/4 or 5/8 meters), the first three eighths (or quarters) are done on one beat (as in faster 6/8 meter), and the following two on a shorter second beat. In 7/8 (or 7/4) meter there are three beats, one long and two short. These beats seem complicated, but they are simple when the conductor has absorbed the articulation. Then his beat will be natural, the complexity of the rhythm not even noticeable to his audience.

Beats can be practiced in class if one student conducts while the class claps: the eighths at first, with the necessary articulation; then, in faster tempo, only the quarters and dotted quarters. A good example may be found in the scherzo of Borodin's Third Symphony (unfinished).* The following, taken from Bartok's *Concerto for Orchestra,* is another. At first have the beats of this excerpt clapped and then use the actual example:

Ex. 73

PLACING OF NATURAL ACCENTS

Before deciding how to beat unusual meters, it is necessary to know exactly where the natural accents should be placed within a measure. A 7/4 meter is usually a combination of 3/4 plus 4/4 meter or vice versa, but in the third movement of Prokofieff's Second Violin Concerto the following pattern appears: . This will have to be beaten in two plus three plus two. The pattern is recommended in Fig. 24.

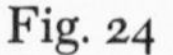

Fig. 24

* The tempo of this movement is so fast that whole measures may even be done on one single beat.

Even a meter that seems normal may consist of different units. The unorthodox accentuation of the rhumba has been mentioned. In Bartok's *Music for Strings, Percussion, and Celesta* a similar pattern may be found: an 8/8 meter in fast tempo, notated $\frac{8}{8}$ ♩. ♩. ♩ .

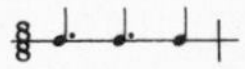

This pattern should be conducted in three, two long beats and one short. It is not meant as a syncopation, as in the rhumba and in Gershwin's *Rhapsody in Blue*; here the three, three, two, is the basic pattern. A similar combination occurs in Barber's *Capricorn Concerto,* but in slow tempo.

In Barber's *Souvenirs* a waltz has a rather unorthodox section in 5/4, and the very unusual 5/4 in the third act of Wagner's *Tristan and Isolde* has previously been mentioned.

Odd meters may be found in Moussorgsky's *Pictures at an Exhibition,* practically all of Stravinsky's works, and the major portion of contemporary music.

The Ear and the Eye

TWO

9

Ear training

EAR training is generally considered "elementary," and therefore unnecessary in a textbook on conducting. This is an error; even an accomplished musician must continue to train his ear, and for a conductor a highly developed "inner" ear is an essential tool. A good conductor must be able to read a score like a book: the better his ear, the greater his mastery over his orchestra.

This is especially important for the leader of a student group. Accomplished musicians seldom play wrong notes, but the less experienced the players, the less likely they are to notice their own mistakes.

The orchestra must play in tune; this is a basic necessity for contemporary music as well as classical, despite a popular belief to the contrary. Although slightly defective pitch may spoil the enjoyment of classical music, the ear of the average listener is accustomed to the harmony. Complex modern music, however, can only be grasped if every note is perfectly in tune. When the orchestra has learned to stay in tune it will be easier for the conductor to discover incorrect notes played by single instruments (see Chapter 23).

To hear such errors and correct them immediately is much more difficult than is generally believed. There is no excuse for failing to hear mistakes in simple classical or romantic music; but if a conductor has only "elementary" ear training he may perhaps hear that something is wrong but be unable to put his finger on it. What follows are four different ways to develop a conductor's ear.

DICTATION

Begin with simple polyphonic and harmonic dictation.

The following exercises start with easy two-part patterns and gradually advance to three- and four-part patterns.

Ex. 74

Ex. 75

Ex. 76

Ex. 77

Ex. 78

Ex. 79

♩=72-112
Ex. 80

♩= 60-96
A
B

C
Ex. 81

♩= 92-120

Ex. 82

♩= 60-96
Ex. 83

These examples should either be played on the piano or sung by members of the class with one or more voices to each part. The remainder of the class should write them down, as in any dictation exercise. In this way sight-singing and dictation are combined. (Future conductors should be capable of singing any instrumental passage that may occur.)

Repeat example 52. Although it is single-lined, it is much more difficult and worth re-examining at this point. It may be a challenge even for advanced students.

As a supplement to dictation, the following procedure is recommended: Sit at the piano and play middle C. Listen to an interval with the inner ear, then play it. When this is mastered, advance to whole melodic lines and phrases, then to two voices and chord progressions – always *thinking* of them before playing. Use printed music (Bach chorales are recommended) but choose unfamiliar examples. Always listen to each chord with the inner ear before playing it. Progress gradually to more and more complicated music. Another useful exercise is to have students write down a familiar song, fully harmonized, from memory without checking up on it beforehand.

RECOGNIZING WRONG NOTES PLAYED INTENTIONALLY

Incorrect notes, if deliberately inserted into the musical exercises in the previous section of this chapter, will provide an excellent ear training test. At first, two or three accidentals should be changed or omitted; in two- and three-part examples change notes in middle and bottom voices as well as accidentals.

RECOGNIZING DIFFERENT INSTRUMENTS

Listen to the following recordings:

SCHUBERT: *Trout* Quintet.
BEETHOVEN: Septet.
MOZART: Serenade in C Minor, K. 388.

HAYDN: Divertimento in B-Flat.
HINDEMITH: *Kleine Kammermusik,* Op. 24, No. 2.
STRAVINSKY: Selections from *L'Histoire du Soldat.*

Then listen to recordings of easier Haydn and Mozart symphonies, gradually advancing to more complicated ones. Write down the instrumentation of each.

Try to identify all the instruments in Ravel's *Bolero.* This is quite difficult, and practically impossible if a good recording and good reproduction equipment are not available.

LEARNING TO READ A SCORE WITH THE INNER EAR

Start with Bach's two- and three-part Inventions (unfamiliar ones). No instrument whatever should be used for this training. The top line should be read with the inner ear for about eight measures. This phrase should be well fixed in the student's memory. Now the bottom line should be read, up to the same point. Adding the two lines together – the one in the student's mind and the one that he reads – should not be difficult. When there are three voices, the two outer voices should be memorized, then put together mentally, and the middle line read. This procedure may seem tedious at first but gradually it should become routine. Eventually the student will be able to read two voices together without having to memorize either. Simple chord progressions should cause no problem. Now the student may proceed to Bach fugues, then to Haydn string quartets, and thereafter to Haydn and Mozart symphonies. Depending upon the ability of the student, more complex scores may gradually be approached.

Should the student try to venture into contemporary music with its highly complicated texture and "atonal" harmony, he may have to return to the initial procedure of memorizing each line separately and then putting them together. If he has absolute pitch, it will be much easier for him. No teacher can actually test a student's progress in this area. The student must judge himself; the final test comes when he stands in front of an orchestra. He must be able to recognize when wrong notes are played and hear exactly which instruments are playing them.

Very often students with manual and interpretative talent have "bad" ears while other students, especially those with absolute pitch, may be "stiff" conductors but have excellent ears. Both groups resent ear-training exercises, the first ones because they get an inferiority complex, the others because they feel ear training unnecessary. This should not deter the instructor. The faculty of hearing correctly is more important than most students realize. Any teacher in an elementary or even high school must avoid the danger of his own ears becoming gradually blunted, having to listen to instruments playing off pitch. On the other hand, it is here where the groundwork must be done. Beginning instrumentalists always have difficulty with pitch, but an instructor's patience can achieve miracles. If he succeeds having an easy piece, preferably a short one, played on pitch, the children's faces will light up, they suddenly feel that they are part of a wonderfully harmonious unity.

10 *Score reading*

AT THE beginning of this century it was virtually impossible for students to own scores of the masterworks. They could only be studied in public libraries. The situation has changed considerably since then. Today almost all important works are available in miniature scores. A student conductor should make it his business to acquire a library of these scores.

The layout of an orchestral score has been standardized since the beginning of the nineteenth century: the woodwinds on top, brass and percussion follow, strings on the bottom. In earlier times, layouts often prevailed with strings above winds. Some works are still only available in the older layout.

In order to read a score — actually read it, not just skim over it — extensive study is needed. First of all, the student has to become familiar with the different clefs used in the orchestra; he should be well versed in reading the alto clef for the viola part and the tenor clef to which, when too many leger lines are needed in bass clef, cello, bassoon, and trombone, parts are switched. These clefs are C clefs; in the alto clef middle C is on the middle line of the staff, in the tenor clef it is on the second line from the top.

Alto clef: Tenor Clef:

Consequently, the middle C of the viola is placed where there would be a B in treble clef — a distance of a seventh; the middle C in the tenor clef is placed where there would be an F in bass clef. This relationship to familiar clefs will be a help to the student when he starts to read the new clefs. As soon as possible, however, he should try to learn to read each clef independently.

TRANSPOSING INSTRUMENTS

Students who have studied orchestration will know about transposing instruments, but a short survey of this subject may be advisable. String basses, contrabassoons, and C horns are not transposing instruments but sound an octave lower, piccolos and celestas an octave higher, than written. Clarinets, trumpets, French horns, *are* transposing instruments: on a B-flat clarinet or trumpet, a written C sounds B-flat; on an F horn a written C sounds F (below); and so on. What sometimes causes a problem is the question whether the instrument transposes up or down. The clarinets range from E-flat down to A, the E-flat sounding a minor third higher than written, the A a minor third lower. *All* horns sound lower than written — the B-flat horn a ninth lower, unless it is specially marked high B-flat (B-flat alto). Of the trumpets only the B-flat and A sound one (or two) steps lower, all other trumpets transposing upward. (The C trumpet is, of course, read as written.) The English horn sounds a fifth lower (like an F horn), the bass clarinet a ninth lower. There are some older scores with bass clarinets written in bass clef: they sound one full step lower than written. Bass clarinets in A may also be found. Today B-flat bass clarinets are written in the treble clef. There is some confusion, furthermore, about the use of the bass clef for horns. In all older scores, horns written in bass clef for some reason transpose upward; the B-flat horn would transpose one step down instead of a ninth, the C horn would be played as written. In twentieth-century scores this usage has been abolished; when horns are written in the bass clef the procedure is the same as in the treble clef. To avoid confusion composers today prefer using treble clef only, even if many leger lines below the staff are needed for low horns.

Bands have a number of additional transposing instruments. They may use the D-flat piccolo (an instrument encountered mainly in England), sounding a minor ninth higher than written. The E-flat alto clarinet sounds a major sixth lower. Once in a while a contrabass clarinet is added (in B-flat) sounding an octave lower than the bass clarinet. All saxophones sound lower than written; the B-flat soprano one full step, the E-flat alto a major sixth, the B-flat tenor a major ninth, the E-flat baritone a major thirteenth (an octave plus a sixth), and the B-flat bass a major sixteenth (an octave plus a ninth).* Bands generally

* In his *Symphonia Domestica* Richard Strauss uses F and C instruments for the saxophone quartet.

have alto, tenor, and baritone saxophones. Cornets transpose in the same manner as trumpets.

Although tenor trombones are B-flat instruments they sound as written; the reason is that without valves (which were invented in the nineteenth century) they could play all chromatic notes. Tubas do *not* sound an octave lower, and neither do timpani; they sound as written.

Today choruses are written in treble and bass clefs only — the tenor part in treble, but sounding an octave lower. In earlier times, however, C clefs were used for all voices except the bass. The soprano clef has middle C on the lowest staff line. Since classical music scores are often available only with the old clefs, students should get used to reading them. This includes composers as late as Brahms; Wagner wrote the tenor parts in C clef while using treble clef for the female voices.

EXERCISES

Start with clef reading, as a preparation for transposing. The tenor clef will equip a student for reading B-flat instruments, the alto clef for D instruments, and the soprano clef for A transpositions. The bass clef is useful for learning to transpose E and E-flat instruments. It is very important, though, to be aware that in transpositions a change in accidentals takes place.

The best clef exercises will be found in old vocal music. Among the great masters of the fifteenth to seventeenth centuries two-part up to five- and six-part works can be found. At first, just one voice in any one of the C clefs should be played on the piano; then original works for two voices; then three, and so on. Modern two- or three-part pieces may be transcribed for the old clefs and assigned to be read at the piano. The soprano clef may be eliminated (the treble clef being kept for the soprano part for the present purpose).*

For an exercise in transposition, start with one voice, preferably a clarinet part — then two clarinets, then two clarinets

* See R. O. Morris and Howard Ferguson, *Preparatory Exercises in Score Reading,* New York, Oxford University Press, 1931.

with one or two bassoons. (Try the beginning of Tchaikovsky's *Romeo and Juliet* overture.) Next, transpose any horn or trumpet part in D, E-flat, E, or A (as frequently encountered in classical music) into F for horns and B-flat for trumpets. Student conductors will find this a valuable ability because a great deal of classical and romantic orchestral material is available only with the original transpositions. In the beginning do the exercise in writing; transpose into concert pitch first, then into the respective F or B-flat.

WRITING CONDENSED SCORES

Extract a written, condensed score from the full score of a masterwork. It should be somewhat like a piano score, but with one difference: it will not be meant for the piano. Each instrument should appear the way it actually sounds; that is, the string bass an octave below the cello, the piccolo an octave higher than written, and all instruments in their natural range. If two or more instruments play identical notes, these should be written only once; if an instrument plays only part of a passage, however, this should be clear. Fill-in harmonies should not be omitted. If the work is organized carefully clutter can be avoided; a well-planned, condensed score should be entirely intelligible.

Ex. 8.

For the beginning, choose scores with strings and no more than four wind parts. In larger scores, doubling voices in different octaves may be omitted by adding "con 8va." The above example (Mozart's *Haffner Symphony*) of a fourteen-voice score is about the limit of what can be done, showing all voices on two staves. A third staff may be added when scores are more complicated.

Writing condensed scores is not actually the job of a conductor, but it is good training. When the student has learned to write well-organized condensations he will be better equipped to visualize the full score, and thus gradually to become aware of its sound with his inner ear.

SCORE READING AT THE PIANO

The student should start with scores of easy string trios by Mozart and Beethoven, sight-reading them at the piano or, if not yet proficient enough, studying them first. (A prospective conductor should be able to play the piano adequately.) Gradually, string quartets should be taken up; then early classical pieces for small orchestra, with two oboes and two horns. Progress will not be fast; score reading at the piano requires many years of practice.

READING A SCORE WITH THE INNER EAR

Training of the inner ear was dealt with in Chapter 9. Skill in score reading should facilitate reading with the inner ear. Both ear training and score reading should be developed simultaneously.

The Instruments

THREE

11 *The strings*

IDEALLY, a conductor should have an inexhaustible knowledge of all the orchestral instruments. Many colleges and conservatories train future music teachers to play at least one instrument from each family. There are, however, only a few very talented musicians who really can master a number of string, wind, brass, and percussion instruments, and to be a good conductor it is not necessary to play them all.

Berlioz, one of the greatest orchestrators, and one of the first professional conductors, could not play any of the standard orchestral instruments well. The same is true of Wagner, the great master of instrument color, who was also an outstanding conductor. On the other hand, great conductors have always zealously studied the scores of the masters, and they have learned the peculiarities of each instrument from listening to and watching first-rate instrumentalists play difficult passages.

The situation is somewhat different in the non-professional field. Here the conductor is part teacher, and must have a more extensive knowledge of each instrument. He must be able to help the student; he must be versed in matters of bowing and fingering in the strings, breathing and fingering in the winds, alternate fingerings, and so on.

In many schools, one teacher-conductor instructs the students in all the instruments of the orchestra. This is not an ideal situation; the conductor should not only have had a course in orchestration, he should be proficient in at least one orchestral instrument in addition to the piano. Preferably, this will be a stringed instrument. Short of that he should acquire a thorough knowledge of all the intricacies of string playing. If a conductor is versed in the different techniques of bowing, the possibilities of fingering, and the manual dexterity needed for playing in tune, he can at least help his students to achieve the right techniques and the right style in playing.

It is impossible to examine in this book *all* the technical and stylistic problems that confront a string player. Below are some of the most important aspects with which a conductor has to cope.

Bowing

LEGATO

Generally, a number of notes are played on one bow. Changing of bows, when necessary, should be done with a minimum of unmusical noises. For this purpose a well-controlled right wrist is important, and when the change of bow occurs within a legato phrase it has to be particularly smooth.

?

Most editions of classical music have the bowings well marked, often added by the editor. This material is printed with a professional orchestra in mind; frequently, students who have not yet achieved the tone necessary for playing long passages in one bow will be unable to use them. There are two ways out of this difficulty. Either mark the parts for more changes of bow, or leave it to the student to use as many bows as he feels necessary. The latter solution has an esthetic disadvantage, since the impression of unity is spoiled. Some audiences may even blame the conductor. On the other hand, a long legato phrase, which youngsters cannot play in one bow, will sound more coherent if the bows are changed at different places. It should not be interrupted by the whole string section at the same point. As in the case of choral singing, to avoid a "breath" in a long legato passage (or on a held note), use the "staggered breathing" technique.

PORTATO – Louré

This is a "borderline" legato bowing and should not be confused with "portamento," which means gliding from one tone to the next. (Except in rare cases marked "glissando" this gliding should be avoided.) Portato is used when a series of repeated notes is to be very smoothly linked: [notation] . A well-known example is the viola accompaniment to the famous second theme in Schubert's *Unfinished* Symphony. In the first movement of Beethoven's First Symphony the romantic concluding theme in the cellos and basses is accompanied in this manner by the other strings.

In order to perform this bowing well, the player should play a smooth legato, allowing the tone to fade out at the end of each note without stopping the bow, then starting the next note by applying very slight pressure. As in the change of bow, the right wrist must be well-controlled but flexible.

Portato should not be confused, either, with staccatos on one bow:

Ex. 85

NON-LEGATO (*detached*)

Passages are often not sustained, but should have clearly marked separate notes and be played with the same bowings by all instrumentalists. Hymns and anthems belong to this category. Every note should get a full bow except when the note value is too short (eighth notes, for instance). The bow should be used from one end to the other except in soft passages, the tone continued up to the change of the bow. Each note, however, should be clearly attacked.

DOWN- AND UP-BOW

Use down-bow on downbeats, up-bow on unaccented beats, pickups, and so forth. This is a rule, but it cannot always be strictly enforced. Problems arise in 3/4 meter, in which downbeats may occur on up-bows or two notes may have to be played on one bow. In that case the bowing has to be interrupted, to make the notes sound as if the bow had been changed. Otherwise, an unintended slur will result.

Examine the following example:

Ex. 86

There are two reasons why this bowing, though feasible, is not ideal. First, the second downbeat coincides with an up-bow, and — according to the melodic inflection — this downbeat is even stronger than the first. (The first measure prepares for the second.) Secondly, the first note in the second measure is held for three eighths, whereas the second note is only one eighth. Using the same amount of bow on both creates the danger of stressing the short note, which is on an offbeat. The following bowing would solve both problems:

Ex. 87

This solution has other flaws. In each bar two beats will need the same amount of bow as one — but the ratio is better than the three-to-one of the first example, and that important second measure now has a down-bow.

The relationship of three-to-one becomes even more important in faster tempo. Example:

"Hooked"

Ex. 88

Here, definitely, the marked bowing is necessary. If the bow is changed on every note, the sixteenths will not only be unnecessarily overemphasized, they will generally lose their rhythmic value. The passage may sound something like this:

Ex. 89

The ♪. ♬ ♪. ♬ pattern is very frequent in any kind of music. Bowings are not usually marked when it occurs because professional musicians are thoroughly familiar with it. For beginners, of course, it must be marked until it is learned. The conductor should insist on this bowing from the very beginning.

BAROQUE MUSIC

The baroque style often requires bowings that are stopped before each succeeding note. Practically all the music of Bach and Handel is of this type. The length of the note and the force of the attack depend upon the character of the piece. Slow pieces, sarabandes for example, should be played in the sustained or detached style mentioned earlier; but interruptions are needed when the tempo increases to something between moderato and allegro—especially in the many dance movements of a suite. The introduction in the *Water Music* suite by Handel (Schirmer, edited by this writer) starts:

Ex. 90a

f (*second time* *p*)

It should be played like this:

Ex. 90b

The bow *remains on the strings*; full bow is used for forte and half for piano. When used in full strength, this bowing is called *martellato* or *martellé* ("hammered"). For soft passages the bowing is similar, but with the hammering eliminated. It is almost like a staccato bowing, although the style should not have the crispness of a real staccato. When the notes follow each other in fast succession there should be no stop after each note; therefore eighths and sixteenths in allegro tempo must be played detached—non-legato, but not staccato.

The bowings in the bourrée of Bach's Suite No. 2:

Ex. 91

An important bowing, somewhat similar to the one mentioned above is used for the following pattern (from Gluck's *At the Court of Maria Theresa*):

mart.

Ex. 92

An interesting example of its use in slower tempo is found in the Loure of the Handel suite:

Ex. 93

Notice that it starts on a down-bow although the first note is on an offbeat.

STACCATO

For a really crisp staccato bowing, the two methods below have been used since the classical period.

The *spiccato* ("bouncing") is generally executed in the middle of the bow, which is held so that it jumps slightly off the string after each tone. Practice is needed for this and beginners often get more noise than tone, but they should learn it as soon as possible. If students continue to play short tones without leaving the string, as in baroque music, they will never get the crispness and elasticity needed. The eighth-note accompaniments found so frequently in classical and early romantic music should always, unless marked otherwise, be played spiccato.

For *saltando* (or *saltato,* "jumping") the bow is lightly thrown onto the strings so that it bounces, thus producing two eighths or a triplet at a speed which would be very difficult to achieve by any other means. (The so-called "flying staccato" is done in a similar manner but involves a whole series of notes. Since it is a technical device used mainly by soloists, it needs no discussion here.) A famous example of the saltando is the last allegro in the *William Tell* overture. The third allegro theme in Schubert's *Rosamunde* overture is also best played with saltando bowing. This technique is not easy and needs even more practice than the spiccato. It is, however, used very much less frequently.

Although saltando notes occur mostly on an upbeat, they are done on a down-bow. The downbeat therefore occurs on an up-bow. In the third movement of his Second Symphony Mahler specifically asks for this bowing (but uses the German term, *Springbogen*).*

OTHER BOWINGS

In waltzes, second violins and violas often have the following pattern:

Ex. 94

Although they start on the weak second beat, they should use a down-bow. To play it with two successive up-bows, as do some players, is less desirable. In the Viennese waltz, where there is usually some emphasis on the second beat, the down-bow is especially appropriate. A light and soft spiccato, if the players are capable of performing it, is preferable to remaining on the strings with short strokes. Routine dance orchestras frequently play this way; it takes all the grace out of the waltz.

Sometimes a succession of two or more down-bows is called for. In the following pattern both down-bows should start at the frog:

Ex. 95

f

An example of the bowing above may be found at the start of Brahms's Sixth Hungarian Dance.

The following passage:

Ex. 96a

* Some conductors recommend an up-bow on a downbeat to achieve special effects. Hans von Bülow had Mozart's G Minor Symphony (see example 123) start on a down-bow. This avoided heaviness on the downbeat, and the whole theme had a more flowing and graceful character. Since then, orchestras have used this reverse bowing in many works, classical and modern. It is not, however, recommended for student groups, unless they are quite advanced.

will have much more vigor and force if done:

Ex. 96b

rather than:

Ex. 96c

This bowing is appropriate at the start of Johann Strauss's *Gypsy Baron* overture.

On the other hand, the pattern 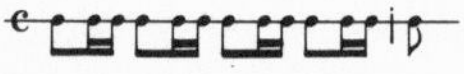 is best bowed  , using long strokes for both down- and up-bows on the eighths, and short strokes at the tip and the frog for the sixteenths. The bow should be kept on the strings throughout. A good example is the allegro in Handel's *Samson* overture.

A succession of chords  should be done with down-bows only. Consecutive down-bows can be found toward the end of the second movement of Mahler's Fifth Symphony, and in Stravinsky's *Petrushka* and *Rite of Spring*.

Start on an up-bow when a sustained passage (or held note) begins very softly, even if it is on a downbeat. Vigorous staccato notes should be played close to the frog, using a strong, but never scratching, spiccato:

Ex. 97

TONE REPETITION

In order to achieve greater sonority, composers often write the string passage:  like this:  . Such passages often sound messy. For the best effect, the strings should play  successive down-bows with as much bow as possible *without* lifting the bow. Naturally, the up-bow between each down-bow will be used, but the player will not be conscious of it and the passage will be sonorous and clear.

This tone-doubling device may be found as early as Haydn and Mozart; Beethoven, who strove for greater sonority, made frequent use of it in the climaxes. Schumann was especially partial to doubling and even tripling and quadrupling, of notes in the strings. In his Fourth Symphony, for example, the allegro in the first movement is written in rather fast sixteenth notes. Schumann doubles even these, producing extremely fast thirty-seconds. He was not a string player and may have overdone it: one more reason to use the method above and avoid a jumbled sound. Later romanticists used the device more sparingly and contemporary composers have gotten further away from it.

Students should be aware that printed bowing and other marks in classical and especially baroque music are seldom the original ones. Most editions of old music have been published for "practical use." The editors may have been good craftsmen, but their work bears the stamp of their own style and their own period (see Chapter 22). Some publishers have recently reverted to printing the unedited original (*Urtext*). These editions are almost void of bowing marks, and it is up to the conductor to add them according to his taste and the technical ability of his group. *Urtext* editions should be used instead of those edited in the late romantic period.

Fingering and related matters

Beginners like to use open strings, especially when avoiding them requires a change in position. Violins and violas do not need to use open strings if they are told to avoid them, but cellos have a harder time in this respect. In basses open strings are fortunately not so conspicuous as in higher instruments; in general, they are preferable to higher-position tones. In the other string instruments compromises have to be made. Students are more inclined to learn a stringed instrument if they can get an early chance to join the orchestra. They will not be able to do so without using open strings; and if they try to avoid them, they may play badly out of tune. The conductor must decide which is worse — the unpleasant sound of an open string, or the sometimes more unpleasant sound that results from trying to avoid it.

PROBLEMS

As soon as the key signature has more than three sharps or two flats, beginners will be apt to overlook the D-sharp or A-flat. Flats are especially awkward for cellos and basses. Players should be trained to know the difference between whole steps and half steps; since the fingering is the same this can be a problem for violins and violas. Cellists and bass players, on the other hand, become aware of the difference from the very beginning, since half and whole steps require different fingerings. Augmented seconds cause a special dilemma to beginners who, in reading the music, often do not realize how far apart the two notes are. Another frequent problem occurs when there is an enharmonic change — say when a D-sharp becomes an E-flat. Some players, seeing the E-flat a step above the D-sharp, fail to realize that the two are (practically) the same note.

Clean playing becomes more and more difficult when string players have to play above third position. Beginners should remain in first position until they have mastered it, and this usually takes quite a while. If the conductor is a string player himself, he will have no trouble in determining which should be the best fingering for his strings. If he is not, he should seek the help of a string teacher or an especially competent player. Few editions contain enough fingering marks: additional ones should be inserted in all string parts. Good fingering will improve the pitch considerably.

Double stops cause difficulty for inexperienced players. Except for very easy ones these should be played "divisi" by beginners; each player must know exactly which part is his. The player sitting on the right side of the stand usually has the upper notes, the player on the left the lower: If this is not made quite clear both will very likely play the top part. When three voices are marked divisi, the notes should be evenly divided among the group.

PIZZICATO

Most students believe that pizzicato is easier than arco – but a good pizzicato is less simple than it seems. The part of the string that comes in contact with the bow must not be touched: the slightest perspiration on the fingers may make the strings greasy and unfit for good bowing. On the other hand, plucking should not be done too close to the pegs: the best place is exactly halfway between bridge and scroll. Fingernails should never be used for plucking.

There are also differences in the kind of pizzicato. Soft pizzicatos should be done by just touching the strings with the fingertips; in a sharp passage the fingertip should pull the string more or less strongly, but never hard enough for the string to hit the fingerboard.

The execution of a pizzicato does not raise as many problems as the use of the bow. Because the pizzicato has a percussive sound, however, any unevenness will be much more obvious to the listener than it would be in a bowed passage. Much depends here on an absolutely clear beat from the conductor.

MUTES

These should always be used when composers call for them. Mutes (also called sordinos) not only decrease the volume, they change the color. Sometimes, if the string group is very small, it may be best for only half the members to use them. Composers do not ask for mutes very frequently, but string players must always have them ready in the event they are needed. They must be put on and taken off very carefully so as not to cause the slightest noise, especially if it has to be done during a rest or very soft passage.

SPECIAL EFFECTS

The expression *col legno* means "with the wood"; it indicates that the player should turn his bow around and play with its back. Done by a full orchestra a rather weird, percussive sound emerges, which may be very effective for special purposes, as in the *Witches' Sabbath* in Berlioz's *Symphonie Fantastique.* One can actually visualize skeletons dancing. The same effect is achieved in Saint-Saëns *Danse Macabre.* Strangely enough, Chopin, a composer who rarely wrote for orchestra, asks for a *col legno* in the last movement of his F Minor Piano Concerto. *Col legno* is frequently found in contemporary music.

For another special effect string parts are marked *sul ponticello* ("at the bridge"). Having the bow glide close to the bridge produces a weird sound, but softer and more mysterious than col legno. Depending upon the way it is done it can seem "icy" or of penetrating sensuality. When Wagner uses this effect in the *Lilac Monologue* in the second act of *Die Meistersinger,* one can almost sense the pervasive odor of the lilac bushes. (Wagner used the German expression *am Steg.*) *Sul ponticello* is generally played tremolo, at the tip of the bow.

In the second act of *Tristan and Isolde* Wagner has *sul ponticello* strings imitate the nocturnal sounds of rustling leaves; and in the final scene of *Wozzeck,* Alban Berg creates a weird impression of the swamp in which Wozzeck drowns himself. Other examples of *sul ponticello* are the song of the will-o'-the-wisp in De Falla's *El Amor Brujo;* the dance of the blackamoor in Stravinsky's *Petroushka;* and a number of passages in *The Rite of Spring.*

Sul tasto ("at the fingerboard") creates a similar effect, but less piercing and rather subdued and hazy. Stravinsky uses it at the dreamy end of the berceuse in his *Firebird,* an excellent characterization of sleepiness. In Debussy's *Afternoon of a Faun* the same effect (here marked in French *sur la touche*) creates a feeling of utter quiescence.

12 *The woodwinds*

THE strings are the backbone of the orchestra, but the conductor must be thoroughly acquainted with the other instruments as well. It takes time to achieve a certain skill on a stringed instrument, but strings generally play in groups and inexperienced players can be "dragged along" by more proficient ones. In orchestral music, woodwind parts are generally written one player to a part, and each player is required to be a soloist. This may even be true of the second voices, which sometimes are called upon to play quite independently. A wind player may be able to join the orchestra at an earlier stage of his studies than a string player, but the fact that each woodwind player must be independent somewhat outweighs this advantage. Only in a band do the winds play in groups (the clarinet section actually replaces the strings of the orchestra). An amateur orchestra player, struggling with an important oboe or clarinet passage, is more apt to spoil a performance than a few weak strings among a number of competent ones. Consequently, a woodwind player must acquire fine musical taste; and if he is not very talented, the conductor (with the help of the woodwind teacher) must patiently try to improve his musicianship.

The woodwind player must be capable of understanding the passage he plays. There are so many subtle differences between just playing the notes and playing them artistically that the following detailed study should be helpful.

BREATHING

A string player is not able to play a long sustained phrase on one bow; he will have to change it, necessitating an interruption, which should be as inconspicuous as possible. This difficulty does not apply to the winds. It should be kept in mind, however, that instrumental music has its origin in singing: the phrasing and breathing of a good singer should provide a guideline. A wind instrument can generally play a much longer line in one breath than a singer is capable of singing, but a long, uninterrupted passage will sound unnatural. It will lose its meaning.

There are ways for a woodwind to inflect its phrases, just as a good vocal line follows the inflection of the words in a song. As there are commas, periods, colons, and question marks in a vocal piece, so there should be pauses of varying length in an instrumental passage. The woodwind player should at least indicate a break, even if he does not need it, where a singer would take a breath. It may be characteristic of modern instrumental style to play a long, sustained, or sweeping phrase without interruption; still, the listener must be able to feel the organization and structure of the melody through the manner in which it is presented by the player.

ARTICULATION

Different devices are used to articulate the different parts of a melody according to its basic organization:

1] At the end of a clearly terminated phrase, a breath is taken. The amount of breath depends on the length of the desired break; sometimes a short, small breath is entirely sufficient.

2] If the phrases in question are so short that taking breath would make the passage sound "asthmatic," then an almost unnoticeable interruption, without taking breath, is required.

3] If no real interruption is wanted but a "non-legato" is in order, "tonguing" should be applied. Tonguing is achieved by inserting a "D" before the note to be attacked. If a sharper accent is desired, a "T" is used.

With this in mind, examine the following example from Beethoven's Second Symphony, second movement.

Ex. 98

The upbeat and measures 1 and 2 should be slightly tongued. (When there is no slur within a legato phrase, these very soft tonguings are needed.) Before measure 3 a barely noticeable interruption should take place, indicating the second part of the phrase. Measure 4: Soft tonguing. Before measure 5: A short breath for the new phrase, and as a help in building up the following crescendo. Before measure 7: A slight interruption, but without tonguing the next attack, since it must be as soft as possible. (The second part does not start immediately after the first; the strings play this period.) Second part, measure 9: Soft tonguing is called for when a slur ends. Measure 10: The rest indicates only a brief stop, not a breath. Measure 12: A full breath is in order to denote the end of the phrase; a good supply of breath will also be necessary for the following crescendo and *sf*. Measure 14: For the *sf* a sharper tonguing (T) is needed. Measure 15: A return to piano, requiring very soft tonguing.

This woodwind passage has been analyzed in detail to show how any solo melody in the winds should be handled. It should be stressed that string bowings ought frequently to be adapted. For instance, martellato bowings should be matched by the winds. They, too, should interrupt after each note. It sounds amateurish when some groups in the orchestra hold notes longer than others.

For a tone in the winds to be similar to the spiccato in the strings a crisp and lightly-tongued staccato is needed. Often a very airy tone is required, especially from the flutes, in pieces like Mendelssohn's *Midsummer Night's Dream* music (overture and scherzo). Here the flutists lightly touch the notes; there is some resemblance to the flying staccato of the strings.

More important still is double and triple tonguing, which is similar to the string saltando. It enables the flutes (and some experienced clarinetists) to play rhythms such as [rhythm notation] and [rhythm notation] in fast tempo. This technique is effected by articulating the following way: Ti-ke-ti – Ti-ke-ti, and Ti-ke-te-ti – Ti-ke-te-ti, etc. Students will not be able to use this kind of device early in their studies – at least not in very fast tempo.

PITCH

One of the greatest problems for the woodwinds, for many reasons, is the matter of pitch. When starting a rehearsal, the instruments are not yet "warmed up": the pitch will generally rise after the instruments have been played a while. The best way to deal with this problem, however, is to make the player improve his ear so that he will notice when he is out of tune. In the beginning only students with absolute pitch will be able to do this; consequently, after a short period of rehearsing, a general retuning should take place. To a lesser degree the strings, too, are apt to change pitch after a warming-up period, especially when a player is using a new string. Eventually players should learn to adjust their instruments during a few measures' rest, while the remainder of the orchestra is playing. It is up to the conductor to develop in his players an awareness of true pitch.

Another influencing factor is the temperature of the rehearsal room or stage and of the instrument itself. This is one reason for having the orchestra assemble at least five minutes before rehearsal time. (See Chapter 23.) Musicians should be discouraged from taking their instruments with them during intermissions. Corridors and other rooms often have different temperatures.

The oboe is considered one of the most reliable instruments in the orchestra, which is why it is the custom to tune to its A. Nevertheless, the A of an amateur oboist may be out of tune; check it with a tuning fork (440-442 vibrations) or an electric tuner.

That the woodwinds all have the right A does not, of course, mean that all their pitch worries are over. Certain ranges of an instrument are often off pitch; flutes and clarinets are apt to go sharp in the lower and upper ranges. (In today's clarinets the lower range is more accurate.) Bassoons have a tendency to be sharp, mostly in the upper register. Also, single tones may be out of tune. (The C-sharps of the oboe are mostly flat. If the tone is forced in loud passages, flutes, oboes, and bassoons may become sharper, while the clarinet may flatten.) These flaws can be remedied by changing the lip position (on the oboe, bassoon, and flute, but not the clarinet).

Some players, aware of these deficiencies, have acquired the habit of overcompensating. Here again, a trained and attentive ear on the part of the conductor is essential.

The tone quality of the various woodwinds must be constantly observed. All instruments are apt to be shrill in their highest ranges, or squeaky, or pinched, if not played expertly. The clarinet is the one instrument that has no difficulty in the lowest tones. But the flutes easily sound breathy, while the oboe and bassoon have trouble achieving soft tones in the lower registers. Such tones should be avoided when possible, which means choosing pieces that do not require them.

CLARINETS

Non-professional clarinetists seldom own more than one instrument, a B-flat clarinet. Because of this, most publishers now issue a B-flat copy of any work, even if it is originally written for an A clarinet. (Still, clarinet players should be trained to transpose.) This is not an ideal situation: Not only has the A clarinet a slightly mellower tone than the B-flat and a range a half tone lower, but what is of greater importance, passages that create no problem for the A clarinet are extremely difficult on a B-flat instrument. An E major scale is easy — even in fast tempo — on an A clarinet, but much more difficult on a B-flat. Every school, college, or orchestral organization should own at least one A clarinet, to be used when the score calls for it.

Clarinetists who play in bands a great deal, especially in dance bands, have difficulty adjusting their tone to the kind needed in a symphony orchestra. Those who also play the saxophone have become accustomed to a tone so different that they will have difficulties with the subtleties of "serious" music. An especially sensitive player may be the rare exception to this rule.

The basset horn, tuned in F, used by Mozart in his later works and by Beethoven in his *Prometheus* ballet, is actually equal in tone to the alto clarinet of today (which is in E-flat). It could reach a couple of tones lower but, in general, basset horn parts may fittingly be played on alto clarinet.

13 *The brass*

MUCH of what has been said about woodwinds – attacks, breathing, phrasing – also applies to brass.

A brass player should in some ways be trained like a singer; his breathing should be anchored in the diaphragm or he will be unable to blow a succession of sustained notes. Very seldom does one hear the following passage in Wagner's *Die Meistersinger*" prelude done as the composer asked, namely *Sehr gehalten,* "very sustained":

Ex. 99

Generally it is played with a clear break after each quarter note. This is precisely what Wagner did not want, as his marking indicates. Without a well-founded breathing technique, the brass – especially the trombones – will be simply unable to play a sustained passage.

On the other hand, in marches, waltzes, and the like, notes should be played short – though not actually staccato – even if no marks to that effect appear in the parts. (See Chapter 21.) Brass players accustomed to playing in bands – especially marching bands – must change their whole approach when playing "serious" music. (See Chapter 15.) If the orchestra lacks strings, the brass has to refrain, even more severely than in a professional orchestra, from playing too loudly.

HORNS

The one instrument that can easily spoil a performance – and this applies even to professional orchestras – is the French horn. With no other instrument can improper breath control do so much damage. If the horn players are not highly competent avoid pieces that have exposed parts for them. A sensitive conductor should be able to help the horns by adjusting his beat to their breathing; if a horn player has not taken the proper breath before a dangerous spot, he will have trouble.

In professional orchestras, horn players today play from the highest to the lowest range of the instrument with equal facility, but high notes do need a slightly different approach from low ones. For this reason, the first (and third) horn should be played by a student at ease in the higher tessitura, and the second (and fourth) by a student more accustomed to lower notes.

Horns are often muted. In the days of the natural horn this was done by inserting the hand into the bell; this device (called "stopping") was mainly used to raise the pitch half a step. Since the introduction of the valve horn, stopping has become unnecessary, but many players still use this procedure, instead of using a special pear-shaped mute. The conductor should see to it that horns, when stopped, are in tune. (When a composer wants to have the horn stopped, he sometimes adds a + to the note.) Muted horns (and trumpets) are often asked to play forte, to obtain a blaring, grotesque quality.

When a horn passage must predominate, and be clearly heard while the rest of the orchestra plays full force, composers indicate this by marking "bells high." This expression fits the other brass instruments better than it does the horns, for when trumpets and trombones raise their bells, they actually will "cut through." Horns, however, must not only be raised, more important for increasing their volume, since in normal position their sound goes backward, their bells must be turned toward the audience.

The heavy brasses, especially the trombones, need frequent admonitions not to drag. Because they are required to take deep breaths they are apt to be late, and fail to notice that they are still inhaling when they should be attacking. This tendency must be very carefully watched.

Brass instruments, especially the trumpets, can make use of double and triple tonguing. Many fanfares or fanfare-like passages depend upon this device. Trumpets must be particularly careful to play such eighths, triplets, or sixteenths most accurately, if they are not to sound blurred.

Care is especially necessary when *fp* appears. This means

exactly what it says: forte, immediately followed by piano, not forte – diminuendo (see Chapters 5 and 19), and not straight forte with the following tone piano. Similarly, accents in a soft passage require light punches and immediate release – like the prick of a pin, not the blow of a hammer.

Valve trumpets and horns have been common since the middle of the nineteenth century. In earlier times composers had to confine themselves to natural trumpets and horns, with their limited number of tones. A study of Beethoven's scores reveals that he would have used trumpets and horns more frequently, had he found available all the notes on the chromatic scale. Felix Weingartner, the noted Austrian conductor, makes suggestions for small changes and additions in Beethoven's scores, contending that the composer would have done so had he been able to use valved instruments. (*Advice for Performances of Beethoven's Symphonies.*) On the other hand, it should be noted that valved instruments have a slightly harsher tone than natural ones. Brass players, therefore, should avoid blaring tones.

OTHER BRASSES

French (and some Italian) composers of orchestral and, above all, operatic music often use the *cornet* (*cornet à pistons*). It is a relative of the trumpet, generally in B-flat, sometimes in A. Its tube is cone-shaped in contrast to that of the trumpet, which is cylindrical. Bands have adopted the cornet as a regular instrument.

Another instrument in the trumpet family, found in bands, is the *Flügelhorn,* which is like a bugle with valves and related to the saxhorn. It is not regularly used in American bands. At the beginning of the nineteenth century it became the signal-horn of the German infantry, and is now frequently encountered in German bands. It is a B-flat instrument.

During the early part of the nineteenth century another brass instrument, called the *ophicleide,* used for low bass parts, became very popular. (It was invented at the end of the eighteenth century.) It may be found in Mendelssohn's overture to *A Midsummer Night's Dream* and *Elijah,* in Schumann's oratorio, *Paradise and Peri,* and in many of the Berlioz overtures.

The ophicleide superseded the *serpent,* a rather coarse bass instrument known as early as the seventeenth century. Mendelssohn used the serpent in the overture, *Calm Sea and Prosperous Voyage.* Both instruments are obsolete today; their parts are played on the tuba.

Another low brass instrument, used in bands, is the *euphonium* (German *Baryton*), belonging to the tuba family. In American bands tubas themselves are generally replaced by sousaphons.

14 Timpani and percussion (harp and keyboard instruments)

IT IS quite untrue that all one needs to play a percussion instrument is a sense of rhythm; or that just a little training is required to play the bass drum, triangle, or cymbals. If a player can count correctly (not such an easy task) he may be able to perform the necessary noises on time, but without training they will still only be noises.

TIMPANI (*kettle drums*)

A timpanist needs an especially sensitive ear to keep his kettle drums on pitch. To produce a good sound on the timpani is not easy; the timpanist should be a regular member of the orchestra and should be well trained, preferably by a specialist.

Timpani sticks generally have felt heads, but for very soft effects sponge ends may be used. Stravinsky, in *The Firebird*, asks for wooden heads. These sound very brittle; for sharp bangs leather heads are just as good, and they do not sound as harsh as wood.

Timpani are seldom used for carrying a theme. Here are some exceptions:

The famous  in Beethoven's Ninth Symphony.

The  in Wagner's *Parsifal.*

The  start of Richard Strauss's *Burleske.*

Today, timpani can be tuned mechanically (with the foot); a shift from one note to another can be accomplished in a fraction of a second. Some composers have used this change to produce something like a glissando – Bartok for example, in *Music for Strings, Percussion, and Celesta,* and Barber, in the *Hesitation Tango* in *Souvenirs.*

It is probably impossible, in a non-professional orchestra, to have a regular player for every percussion instrument. Some instruments (tom-tom, chimes, tambourine, wood block) are rarely called for. Still, ideally, there should be two percussionists available who play a number of instruments.

SNARE DRUM

This is another instrument that can be played well only by musicians who have had special instruction, and who have a talent for it. It requires a light, precise wrist motion. Composers are usually very exact about snare-drum effects. These may be marked in any of the following ways:

These patterns should be clearly performed. There is a tendency on the part of some percussionists to improvise grace notes. This should not be permitted.

Be sure percussion instruments are in good condition. Timpani and drum tops should be well and evenly stretched. Saving money in this respect is as detrimental to good sound as would be cheap string or wind instruments. False economy does not pay.

Since percussion instruments are mainly used for accentuation and color, great care should be taken to have them follow all dynamic markings. Timpani starting on a piano, followed by a gradual crescendo, are apt to increase volume too early. Percussions, more than any other instruments, should husband their strength and "let go" only at great climaxes. Then their power can vastly intensify a stirring fortissimo.

CYMBALS

Cymbals should not be struck horizontally, which cuts off reverberation; they should be "sliced" vertically, which allows them to continue sounding.

Sometimes a composer will desire cymbals played together with the bass drum, as is done in marching bands, with one cymbal attached to the top of the drum. In such cases the score specifically requires this effect.

For the xylophone, of course (as for the glockenspiel, vibraphone, and marimba), special training is needed. The celesta can be played by any pianist.

PIANO

Although the piano is generally considered a solo instrument, contemporary composers have begun to use its bell-like or percussive sounds in the orchestra. Strauss's opera, *Ariadne auf Naxos,* is composed for a small orchestra with every voice playing soloistically, including the piano. Stravinsky uses the piano in two ballets, *Firebird* and *Petroushka.* In his little opera-sketch, *There and Back,* Hindemith employs three pianos with winds. The score of Menotti's *Medium* asks for piano four hands with small orchestra. These are just a few examples from the modern literature. The harpsichord, the predecessor of the piano (originally called *pianoforte*), played an important part in the orchestra up to the end of the eighteenth century. The conductor sat at the harpsichord and conducted from there, playing the figured bass from the score.

HARP

The harp was played in the Egypt of the Pharaohs. Since then it has, of course, undergone many changes. The double-pedal harp was invented at the end of the eighteenth century. After a few decades the masters of the romantic period became acquainted with the possibilities of this instrument, and since then the harp has been used to add new colors to the orchestral palette. From Berlioz on, French music is full of important harp passages. Brahms used it in his *German Requiem* and Bruckner in his Eighth Symphony. Tchaikovsky's *Romeo and Juliet* overture and his ballets are scored for splendid harp effects. There are few works of Mahler, Strauss, or Debussy without a harp.

The conducting student should at least know how a double-pedal harp works. It is tuned diatonically, in C-flat major. Each of the seven pedals can raise each of the seven tones of the scale a half step or a full step (simultaneously in all octaves). With the pedals halfway down the key is C major; all the way down it becomes C-sharp major.

All kinds of glissando combinations can be achieved on the harp. For one example, the pedals are set as follows: C-flat, D (a half step up), E-sharp (a full step up), F, G-sharp (a full step up), A-flat, B (a half step up). In this line-up E-Sharp and F, and G-sharp and A-flat, are identical. In a glissando these notes would thus be played twice, but a glissando moves so fast that the double notes would not be noticed. What will be heard is a diminished seventh.

Here are a few examples with other glissando combinations:

DEBUSSY: *Prelude to the Afternoon of a Faun* (half-diminished chord).
RAVEL: *Le Tombeau de Couperin* (pentatonic scale).
PROKOFIEFF: *Alexander Nevsky* (pentatonic scale).
STRAVINSKY: Berceuse from *The Firebird* (whole tone scale).

ORGAN

For performances of sacred music, the organ is often combined with the orchestra. One purely orchestral work incorporating the organ, Saint-Saëns's Third Symphony in C minor, is well known.

The organ is such a complicated instrument that a detailed explanation of the way it functions would go far beyond the scope of this book. When a conductor is called upon to augment his orchestra with an organ, certain problems may arise. He must be able to see the organist and vice versa, and this may not be easy. Very often mirrors are needed. Furthermore, organ and orchestra often do not blend. It may be necessary to make a tape recording in order to give the conductor a chance to change the balance.

15 *Balance of tone*

ONLY since the romantic era have composers used different dynamic marks and terms such as "espressivo," "cantabile," or "marcato" to indicate which voice should lead. In the classical period all parts were marked equally; it was up to the conductor to balance the orchestra and bring forth the important voices.

Mendelssohn was one of the first composers to give different parts entirely different dynamic signs. In the *Midsummer Night's Dream* overture he marks a horn attack *ff* while the rest of the orchestra plays *pp*. Slight differences in dynamic signs may also be found in Schubert's *Unfinished* Symphony (see *Workbook*), composed four years before Mendelssohn's overture.

The late romanticists, from Wagner to Strauss, were most meticulous in their scores, indicating exactly which instruments were to predominate. Horns were asked to turn their bells forward, trumpets and trombones to lift them, in order to increase their volume. The climax of this meticulous marking was reached in the works of Mahler. Among contemporary composers, the neoclassicists seem to be returning to the earlier one-dynamic pattern.

It is the conductor's job to achieve the right balance of tone through diligent rehearsals. He has to make the players understand that there is no standard piano or forte. They have to be taught to play with open ears; they must learn what their role is in the ensemble, and that they have to adjust their intensity of tone to it; often it is not the loudness that counts but the intensity.

A forte in some instruments, imperiling transparency and covering leading voices, can be modified by a strong attack with a quick release – a kind of *fmf*, or in powerful climaxes, *ff-f*. In legato passages, these instruments must be advised to hold the *mf* after the *f* up to the next note. (There is apt to be a diminuendo or even a break before the next tone.) For these balancing purposes the conductor should "edit" all orchestral parts.

Some leaders, however, overdo matters by their constant endeavor to have the principal voice predominate.* *Every* voice is

* Some pianists, when playing fugues, overemphasize the entrance of each voice and reduce the counterpoint to a minimum. It is as if the performer were pointing a finger each time and saying: "Listen, this is the theme."

important. Even a pure accompanying passage should not be so subdued that it is not clearly heard.

A good example of how a conductor must balance the tone is in the last movement of Beethoven's First Symphony. The second violins, played as written, will not be clearly heard (see *Workbook*). A similar example is Beethoven's Fifth Symphony:

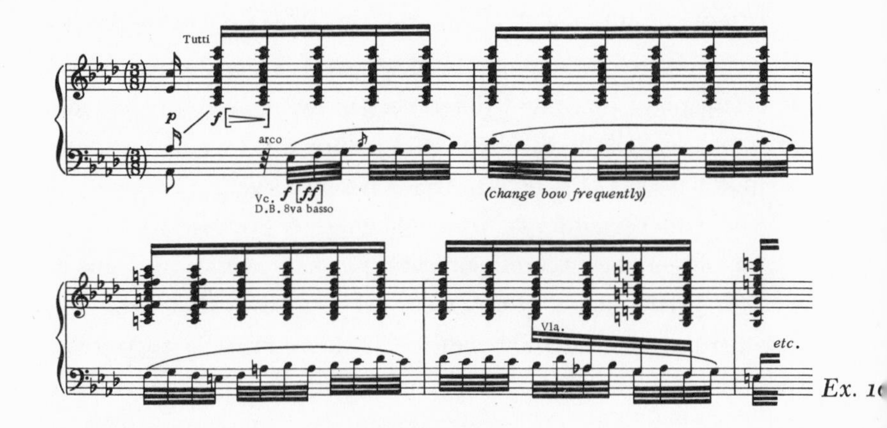

Ex. 10

Above, the bass parts must be clearly heard. Modifications in the other voices will be necessary.

In an interesting example (101), the first measure and a half trumpets help to carry the melody. At the end of the second measure violins, oboes, and clarinets continue in the middle register. The trombones, playing a secondary part in their best range, are apt to drown out the melody if not held back.

Another good example is the start of Weber's *Euryanthe* overture. Here the brass has to hold back in order to let the strings cut through, especially while they play in a low range.

In classical, romantic, or contemporary music, woodwinds (or brass, or both together) often hold a single note for a full measure or longer. This happens frequently at the end of a piece. If composers were aware of stronger and weaker ranges in the different instruments and arranged the combination accordingly, this would result in balanced harmony. But this is not always the case. In a student group, furthermore, the tone capacity of the different instruments may vary considerably. It is here that the conductor must balance the harmony so that no single tone predominates and none is too weak.

When working with non-professionals, other problems will arise. Important instruments may be entirely missing; some sections — very often the strings — may be too weak. The young

15
Balance of tone

Ex. 101

conductor, taking over such an orchestra, must do his best with what he has, trying to improve matters gradually. When sufficient funds are available, a few professionals should be engaged, at least for concerts. Competent musicians can be a tremendous boost to the spirit of the group.

If the players at hand are in their primary stages, if balance of tone is impossible to achieve – not to mention other shortcomings –if it is a conglomeration that just never can sound like an orchestra, the young conductor has an up-hill fight on his hands. To start with, the kind of music should be used that lends itself best to this type of orchestra. Substitute instruments may be employed (see Chapter 16). There are editions for young players on the market. Choose them with discrimination.*

Many beginners' editions have one weakness in common: practically all instruments – strings, winds, brass, and percussion – play from beginning to end, without a rest. What a boring sound! There is of course a reason for this "arrangement": when many instruments play the same part, the weak ones will be carried along by the stronger ones. Also, children all want to play and not sit there and count rests.

A competent teacher should find a way out. He will know which of his youngsters play adequately. He will ask the violins, for instance, to play the melody in the first four or eight measures, then have a clarinet take over. When he builds his orchestra gradually, the teacher may contrast the wind group with the strings or brass and thus achieve a varied orchestral tone.

There is an edition – often used in elementary schools – that has the melody in all parts except the bass. Each part also has an accompanying voice. Of course, all youngsters want to play the melody, so it will happen that in *Silent Night* strings, winds, and brass all play the tune! The students may have fun doing it, but musical taste cannot be developed that way. Imagine each mem-

* Editions arranged by this writer try to help; they have added simplified string parts which make it possible for beginners to join the group. For additional suggestions see Appendix.

ber of a football team wanting to carry the ball all the time. Actually, each player has a necessary job, but only *one* can carry the ball. This concept of teamwork is apt to convince youngsters, even when applied to the orchestra. They will be amazed at how much better their group will sound.

16 *Substitution of instruments*

IN THE process of building an orchestra that may not have all the required instruments, substitutes may be needed. Youngsters eager to join may play saxophones, accordions, or guitars. These instruments are customarily not employed in an orchestra, but a way may be found to make use of them.

SAXOPHONE

Some school editions add saxophone parts to substitute for cellos. They are not a suitable alternative. The saxophone tone does not blend well with strings. It is true that cellos are often lacking in an elementary orchestra, but there is no other instrument that can really replace them. The young conductor should, therefore, make every effort to build a cello section – it is of the utmost importance. Only in an emergency should a saxophone be used, and when using it the conductor should be aware that it is less than a substitute; it is almost a calamity.

The saxophone is better suited to replace the horn. The tone, when produced without the wailing and howling effect generally heard in popular music, can blend well with the horn tone. One horn and one alto saxophone can in fact be made to resemble a two-horn combination. Another horn substitute, generally only used in bands, is the mellophone. Its tone resembles that of the horn more closely than does the alto saxophone's. An alto saxophone may, in an emergency, replace an English horn.

The tenor saxophone may be used in place of the bassoon, although it does not have so low a range. Again, coarse sounds should be avoided.

Many school orchestras have no oboe. It is an important instrument. Until an oboe player is developed (which is not easy, because the oboe is one of the most intricate woodwind instruments), it may have to be replaced by a clarinet. The peculiar tone color will be missing, of course, but in many works the oboe part cannot be eliminated. The clarinetist will have to transpose, which in itself is good training. If he is not capable of transposing, the conductor will have to write out the transposed part.

In substituting for a bassoon the bass clarinet is preferable to the tenor saxophone, although its range also is not low enough. A clarinet player will have little trouble switching to a bass clarinet. Its tone is softer and mellower than either the tenor saxophone or the bassoon.

ACCORDION

Considerable discretion should be shown in using the accordion, but there are occasions when it can be called upon. It may be quite suitable in Spanish and Slavic dances. The part must be written out. The conductor should acquaint himself with how an accordion is used and notated for, and especially what harmonic combinations are possible.

There is one instance in classical literature where an accordion is the best choice: in Mozart's German Dance, K. 602, No. 3, a *Leier* is called for. This is a hurdy-gurdy, an instrument that was later replaced by the barrel organ. If there is no hurdy-gurdy available the accordion comes closest to this sound.

GUITAR

Another instrument seldom used in the orchestra but frequently played by youngsters is the guitar. The guitar is one of the oldest musical instruments and great Spanish music has been written for it. Today it is mainly employed to accompany folksongs, and — often electrically amplified — it has become an important instrument in dance bands. The fact that it has a certain tonal resemblance to the harpsichord makes the guitar suitable for baroque music. It should play the continuo part, written out for the guitar player by the conductor who will thus have an opportunity to learn guitar technique.

The guitar is also suitable for folk dances, Spanish and Italian, as well as the Austrian waltz, the mazurka, the csardas, and the gopak. The csardas employs a cimbalon (dulcimer), the gopak a balalaika, both of which have a guitar-like sound. The banjo would be still closer to the harsher tone of these instruments.

The mandolin is less adaptable to orchestral sound because of its tinkling quality and constant tone repetition. Nevertheless, the conductor with a sense of orchestral color might use it for the melody in Italian folk and dance music. He would, of course, be lacking in taste if he permitted the mandolin to double the melody throughout.

RECORDER

The recorder has again become very popular, especially with young people. It is not a good substitute for any instrument in the orchestra – not even the flute. Since the middle of the eighteenth century, when recorders were still used in small ensembles, the tone volume of the orchestra has increased considerably. Today, the thinness of the recorder tone, its lack of overtones, would cause it to be lost in the orchestra. It is an instrument for intimate chamber music, and students who play recorders should not be discouraged from continuing to use them. They should get together and play – apart from the orchestra – some of the many charming ensemble-pieces available, preferably with the accompaniment of a harpsichord or spinet, or with guitar or piano.* Meanwhile these students should receive training in other instruments, either strings or woodwinds. Strings are desperately needed in school orchestras, but woodwinds have fingerings similar to those of recorders.

It should be the ambition of any conductor to eliminate gradually these substitute instruments. It is here that his initiative and enthusiasm can bring results unexpected by students and school administration.

* There are relatively inexpensive harpsichords and spinets on the market that lend themselves extremely well to playing in small ensembles. They are practically indispensable for baroque chamber music. They blend well with recorders, flutes, oboes, and single strings. Baroque music affords an invaluable training ground for the young instrumentalist, and with the right kind of electrical amplification these small instruments may even be suitable for the continuo part of old music in larger orchestral performances.

Interpretation

FOUR

17

The basis: adherence to the letter of the score

RICHARD WAGNER criticized the "time-beaters" of his generation and stressed "interpretation" as a conductor's main job. This was at the climax of emotionalism during the romantic period. After Wagner, a conductor was judged by the amount of individuality and originality he put into his work. Those who saw and heard Bülow and Nikisch have testified to their unorthodox interpretations. These conductors took liberties with the scores of the masters, but they undoubtedly achieved exciting and unusual performances.

Our own century has turned away from romanticism. One of the great conductors of this century, Arturo Toscanini, established a new interpretive conception, namely, doing the score "as is." His ideal was to adhere as closely as possible to the original. He did away with changes of tempo and dynamics not called for in the score. He showed that a conductor can do an inspiring job without "interpretation." A highly sensitive musician and efficient conductor should be able to unveil all the hidden mysteries in the scores of the masters without resorting to emotionalism and even tricks, just for purposes of effect.

The conducting student – in the beginning at least – would do well to forget about "individual interpretation" and follow Toscanini's example. Only after he has absorbed all the minute details of a score, approaching it with a searching mind to find its hidden voices and meanings, has he the right to "interpret" it "his" way. And if he *is* a good musician, he will discover that the work as it is written – if it is a masterwork – will not need special interpretation. His next task is to have his orchestra play exactly what the composer asks for – which is not an easy task. The young conductor should – if possible – attend rehearsals of a good orchestra. He will discover that a very competent conductor is needed – even with a professional group – to see to it that every note is played exactly as written. It is all the more imperative to have a painstaking leader for a non-professional orchestra.

NOTE VALUES

The mainstay of conducting is precision. The first chapters of this textbook dealt with the problems of precise attacks. Equally important is the matter of accurate note values. Every note must be held exactly as long as its value requires. Inaccuracies in this area result not only from carelessness but also from lack of understanding of orchestral style. One of the most common mistakes is the failure to realize that an eighth note in a slow movement may be rather long, especially if the time is beaten in slow eighths. When in such movements quarter notes occur, they should be held two full beats and released exactly on the start of the third.

Beethoven's Second Symphony, second movement:

Ex. 102

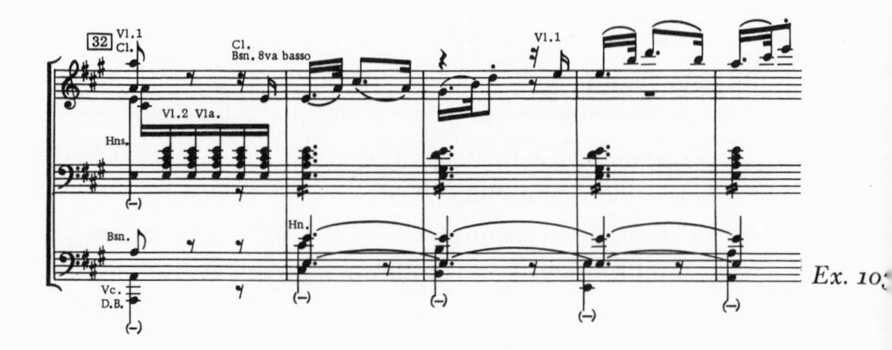

Ex. 10

17

Adherence to the score

Beethoven's Third Symphony, Funeral March:

Hold the quarter up to the downbeat of measure 21.

One often hears Schubert's *Unfinished* (the first dramatic attack) done the following way:

instead of

For a similar reason, in this author's edition of Gluck's *Don Juan* overture, the parts are specifically marked:

in order to induce players to give the quarter notes their full value.

Excellent examples may be found in many of Handel's works. If all notes are clearly cut off, precisely at the right moment, the power and grandeur of his music will be enhanced.

OFFBEAT NOTES

These need special attention. The orchestra will be praised for its "professional" approach if it is trained from the very beginning to play them accurately. Precision in orchestral playing is at least as important as technique.

In the following passages: and , the eighth notes are often played so fast they do not receive their full value. Furthermore, one frequently encounters: and with the eighth notes "dropped." In order to counteract this, have the musicians (for the beginning at least) play these passages like this: and .

EXAMPLES:

A] MOZART: *Eine Kleine Nachtmusik,* start.
SCHUBERT: Ballet music from *Rosamunde,* start.

B] BEETHOVEN: Second Symphony, second movement, mm. 128-137.
BACH: Violin Concerto in E Major, start.
BACH: Suite No. 3, first movement, vivace.
BACH: Piano Concerto in D Minor, last movement.

The beginning of the march in Verdi's *Aida* has the following rhythm: . Draw the orchestra's attention to the two sixteenth notes; have them done exactly on time and exactly as strong as the notes *on* the beats. The improvement should be obvious. The march will have the true Verdi vigor.

A pitfall for any orchestra is the following rhythm: The eighths are apt to be rushed. The tie is held so long that the following three eighths start late, sounding almost like a triplet. Care should be taken that the first of those three eighths is exactly on time. The orchestra should realize that the articulation is: [rhythm] and not: [rhythm] .

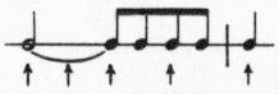

Examples of this pattern are:

> HAYDN: *London* Symphony, first main theme.
> GLUCK: *Don Juan* overture, the sixteenth pattern.
> SCHUBERT: *Rosamunde* overture, allegro, first forte passage.

In the finale of Beethoven's Fifth Symphony (ninth measure) the following pattern occurs in the trumpets: [rhythm] If they take a breath before the three eighths they are apt to be late.

Another rhythm problem: [rhythm] . This has been dealt with in Chapter 11. When it appears in the winds, it should be tongued sharply unless a sustained tempo is called for.

When this rhythm turns up within a slur, as in the familiar theme of Schubert's *Unfinished,*

Ex. 108

the eighths as well as the sixteenths may not, unless care is taken, be given their full value. They are often played too fast and not distinctly enough.

Another rhythm with which beginners have difficulty is derived from the old siciliana (a dance), and used frequently in baroque music: [rhythm] or [rhythm] (For the most precise bowing of this pattern see Chapter 11.) A suitable starting exercise for this rhythm is *Silent Night*, done in a soft legato. The first movement of Beethoven's Seventh Symphony uses this rhythm throughout, but in faster tempo. If the orchestra is not well disciplined, it may gradually lose the rhythmic precision and play [rhythm] instead of [rhythm] .

Additional examples:

GLUCK: *At the Court of Maria Theresa,* siciliana (slow), and finale (faster).
BIZET: *L'Arlésienne* suite, middle part of *Carillon* (moderately slow).
SULLIVAN: *Mikado,* The Flowers That Bloom in the Spring.
WAGNER: *Ride of the Valkyries.*
FRANCK: *Le Chasseur Maudit* (*The Cursed Hunter*).
TCHAIKOVSKY: Fifth Symphony, first movement.

An orchestra is often inaccurate when different values apply to similar patterns. (See page 149: Beethoven's Fifth Symphony, second movement. In the fourth measure there is a thirty-second upbeat, in the next a sixteenth.) In *The Proud,* from Dittersdorf's *Tournament of Temperaments,* there is this pattern: If neglected, it could be played: . Passages of this type are found frequently.

When a conductor draws the attention of his players to such subtle differences it shows that he knows his function and has scrupulously studied his score.

Strict adherence to the letter of the score will not, however, *always* insure a correct performance. In Chapter 5 it was shown that cross rhythms seldom occur in baroque music; when they occur dotted eighths and sixteenths should be adjusted to triplets. There are other instances in baroque music of a similar nature.

In the chorus *Surely He Hath Borne Our Griefs,* in Handel's *Messiah,* the following combination occurs in the original:

It should be played: which is the way it now appears in most editions.

This brings up still another modification. The following pattern: or (this one occurs in the overture to *The Messiah*) has traditionally been played: or: . Many eighteenth-century writers (among them even Leopold Mozart, Wolfgang's father, in his textbook on violin playing) recommend this procedure. The elder Mozart contends that, if played as written, this pattern would sound "boring." The shortened note is certainly capable of making the rhythm sharper. Since the eighteenth century, however, orchestra technique has improved considerably. If the sixteenths (or eighths) are slightly accentuated and played with utmost precision, playing this pattern as written will sound anything but boring. It is up to the taste of the conductor either to adhere to the letter of the score or to follow tradition and change the one dot to two. The important principle is to have the pattern done one way or the other by every member of the orchestra. The conductor must have a clear conception of what he wants to have done, and if he decides to play this pattern the traditional way – changing the one dot to two – he should either announce it to the whole orchestra and have them make the alteration or, better still, have the parts corrected in advance of any rehearsal.

The usual meaning of "interpretation" actually has not been touched upon in this chapter. With reason. If a conductor insists, before trying to give the work his personal touch, that every note be played *correctly*, he will find that the substance of "interpretation" has been realized.

18 *Tempo*

ONE OF the most important and controversial aspects of musical interpretation is the choice of the "right" tempo.

Today, when there are so many different versions of the same selection recorded by the greatest orchestras under the greatest conductors, there is a recognition that there does not seem to be one "right" tempo. Each selection is played at a different speed on each recording. Although differences may be almost unnoticeable in some instances, often they are quite considerable.

This should be surprising. It does seem reasonable to believe that, the composer having indicated the tempo with what are supposed to be unmistakable markings, performances would be fairly uniform.

MARKINGS

In fact, markings are not at all unmistakable. The inaccuracy is shown in the following list, which explicates the well-established tempo marks.

allegro	Fast, not so fast as vivace or presto.
*allegretto**	Not so fast as allegro, with a light touch.
andante	At a slowly moving pace. (The greatest discrepancies arise here, depending upon whether the emphasis is on slowly or moving.)
adagio (*largo*, *lento*)	Slow and sustained.

These are the basic tempo marks. Composers use additional words or phrases as modifications of these tempos, such as:

ma non troppo, or *moderato*	Not too much, or moderate.
(*più*) *mosso*, or *con moto*	Moving, indicating a slightly faster speed.

* This is a diminutive of allegro. Other diminutives, such as adagietto, larghetto, andantino, are used in a similar way: they modify the tempo. Allegretto is slightly slower than allegro, whereas larghetto is somewhat faster than largo. The fact that andantino is faster than andante indicates that andante is rated as a slow tempo.

poco	A little, which generally modifies più (more) or meno (less) mosso.	
molto	Much.	
sostenuto	Sustained.	
vivace	Lively	Usually in connection with allegro.
con brio	With vigor	
con fuoco	With fire	
assai	Considerably.	
cantabile	In a singing manner.	
expressivo	With expression.	
maestoso	Majestically.	

Schumann often used German markings, believing he could be more exact that way. In his romantic exuberance he once wrote "*So schnell wie möglich*" (as fast as possible), and later in the same piece "*Noch schneller*" (still faster). Despite his linguistic inconsistency performers know what Schumann meant. He wanted an almost impossibly fast tempo.

When J. N. Mälzel invented the metronome, Beethoven was one of the first composers to make use of it to indicate exactly the tempo he wanted. But some of his metronome marks are misleading. For instance, the finales of the Eroica and Seventh Symphonies are marked so fast that, if done that way, they would be unduly rushed. The opening of the finale of the Ninth Symphony would result in chaos.

Thus Beethoven's own markings cannot be trusted. He inserted the M.M. (Metronome Mälzel) indications when he was already rather deaf, and imagined tempos will often be quite different from the tempos one uses when working with an orchestra.

Nevertheless, some of Beethoven's indications are helpful. It is better to have them than no M.M. markings at all. Italian tempo markings alone can be so vague they become practically useless. There is an example of this in the trio in the scherzo of the Seventh Symphony. The scherzo runs along at a fast pace — Beethoven marks it 𝅗𝅥. = 126. In the trio he asks for "assai meno mosso" — considerably slower. How much is "considerably"? It is generally played at 𝅗𝅥. = 52-60. Toscanini, however, conducted it at about 𝅗𝅥. = 84, which still is "considerably" slower than 𝅗𝅥. = 126.

TEMPO AND TEMPERAMENT

When comparing Toscanini's version of the minuet in Mozart's *Jupiter* Symphony with Beecham's, one notices that Beecham plays it at almost half the speed; he emphasizes the old-fashioned dance whereas Toscanini plays it somewhat like a scherzo. Yet it is marked neither moderato nor allegro but allegretto, which in connection with a minuet is a pretty clear indication of the tempo.

The choice of tempo, then, is not only a matter of taste, but of temperament. Toscanini simply could not conduct this minuet in the delicate eighteenth-century style Beecham liked.

The "right" tempo of a minuet has often been a controversial issue. Wagner, in his essay *About Conducting*, complained about the fast tempo generally used for the third movement of Beethoven's Eighth Symphony, marked "tempo di menuetto." According to Wagner, Mendelssohn played it much too fast. Of course, today we do not know how either of them conducted it. Wagner, however, became such a supreme authority that no conductor dared to ignore his recommendations. Consequently, this "tempo di menuetto" was often done at a tempo so slow that it lost its dance-like character and sounded more like music for heavyweights entering a boxing ring. (Beethoven's own marking: MM♩ = 126 indicates a rather fast minuet tempo.)

These examples show how flexible tempo can be. Students who have heard a masterwork performed by a specific conductor, either live or recorded, tend to become accustomed to his tempo; when they hear the piece done by another conductor in a different tempo they call it a "misinterpretation." A good musician may sometimes use an unusual tempo, but not a "wrong" one. One has to be willing to accept different ideas about the speed of a piece.

ANIMATION

The character of a performance is not necessarily a question of tempo. Sometimes a slower tempo sounds faster, and vice versa.* Much depends on the manner in which the piece is played. If an orchestra is not capable of playing fast enough, utmost precision and accentuation – where stylistically possible – may often replace speed. This fact is an important one for conductors of nonprofessional orchestras.

Similar observations pertain to slow tempos. An adagio, played very broadly but with intensity, will hold the listener's interest. Played faster but lacking intensity, it will sound "dragged."

RUBATO

During the romantic period, conductors emphasized expression above all. Fluctuation of tempo was one of their favorite means. Richard Wagner, in *About Conducting* uses his own *Meistersinger* prelude to illustrate his rubato recommendations. But he also gives advice on rubato in earlier, more classical music. If any conductor followed these suggestions today, he would be severely criticized.

Music, and its interpretation, has turned to antiromanticism. Toscanini, on the other hand, although in strict compliance with the wishes of the composer, was too much of a musician to play any score with a mechanically inflexible beat. A careful study of his recordings will disclose that in any expressive passage, or for purposes of clarity or phrasing, there are constant – if barely noticeable – fluctuations of tempo. These represent living, pulsating music, not pure mechanics. Nowadays interpretations are

* Fritz Kreisler, for instance, played the last movement of the Mendelssohn Violin Concerto much slower than is the custom, but he emphasized the staccato character of this movement. In this way the finale had a very crisp, pulsating rhythm, not as elflike but perhaps more exciting. At any rate, the tempo *seemed* fast. The listener did not get the impression of its being played slower than the more virtuoso style of violinists who play this movement at breakneck speed.

often heard that, in order to avoid emotionalism, are so inflexible in tempo that they sound automatic.

The student conductor should, at least in the beginning, avoid rubatos and use a steady tempo throughout. If he is a good musician he will, after some time and experience, apply rubatos instinctively. (See Chapter 20.)

There are also "bad-habit" tempo changes. A tendency to accelerate during a crescendo or slow down on a diminuendo should be firmly checked, unless asked for by the composer. Sometimes, it is even preferable to retard slightly before a dynamic climax — but here again, too much, too obviously, is bad taste.

ENDINGS

It has been the custom to slow down at the end of a piece, but this should not become a fixed procedure. The last measures are very important. The performance may have been spirited; should the ending fall flat, the entire impression will be spoiled and the audience let down. The final measures, therefore, require careful study. An analogy from everyday life: when walking, riding, or driving, one usually slows down before coming to a stop. At other times, however, one may even speed up — or stop abruptly.

Suggestions concerning the endings of standard works:

BACH: Suite in B minor:
In every movement a *slight* broadening in the last two or three measures is appropriate; however, some conductors of today remain in strict tempo up to the last note. (Equally true in most of Handel, who usually indicates a retard.)

MOZART: G Minor Symphony:
1] No change of tempo; a slight emphasis on the last three chords.
2] Practically no change of tempo.
3] Minuet; a very slight broadening may be justified.
4] Finale; no noticeable change of tempo; only emphasis on the last two bars.

BEETHOVEN: First Symphony:

1] No change of tempo; a slight emphasis on the last three chords.
2] An almost unnoticeable broadening may be justified in the last two measures.
3] Minuet; no change of tempo.
4] Finale; again, strictly in tempo.

SCHUBERT: *Unfinished* Symphony:

1] No change of tempo.
2] Very slight change; emphasize the two sixteenths in sixth measure before the end, then remain in this *slighty* slower tempo.

These are examples of different styles. In baroque music a slowing down toward the end (within limits, of course) seems appropriate; in classical and romantic music this is much less often the case. In romantic music the composer often indicates a ritardando during the last measures: but these slow-ups should not be overdone. Some, although unmarked, have even become a fixed tradition.

The last chords of the overtures to Weber's *Der Freischütz* and Wagner's *Tannhäuser* are usually done much more slowly than the main tempo. Neither composer asks for a ritardando at this place; a *slight* broadening may seem appropriate but not an entire change of tempo.

There is apt to be a fermata on the last note of movements that have fast and sweeping endings: a slight hesitation before this last fermata is appropriate, as if taking breath for a last, decisive blow. The last note of Beethoven's Fifth Symphony is a good example.

The student can find additional interesting endings that are worthy of discussion. Many will resemble those examined above, but new ideas may come up to suggest different solutions. Endings with printed ritardandos should be included.

Wagner's *Flying Dutchman* overture, written allegro con brio, uses Senta's ballad as a second theme, marked andante. This is an entirely new tempo, less than half as fast. Later, in a kind of development, the first tempo is even speeded up (stringendo); at the climax the second theme reappears, marked "un poco ritenuto" by Wagner. Generally, conductors revert here to the andante tempo of the original second theme. It is not likely that Wagner would have marked it as he did had he wanted that. Since this passage occurs four times within a short section the tempo would continually shift between very slow and very fast, unduly interrupting the flow.

THE METRONOME

It is good for any conductor to acquire a sense of the time values of different metronome indications. In the beginning the student should use the metronome to check the accuracy of his tempo. At rehearsals the second hand of a wrist watch may be substituted. Eventually, pieces familiar to him can serve as a starting point, as he gradually acquires independence. Marches, waltzes, minuets, or any other kind of music, slow or fast, for which he has an unmistakable sense of time, will serve the purpose. His certainty about the exact tempos of these pieces — tempos he has checked with the metronome — will help him adapt the tempo of any composition to the ones with which he is familiar. This is a slow process, but a worthwhile one.

EXERCISES

From a piece being played on the piano, or from a recording, determine the exact tempo in metronome beats. Next, from a piece being played on the piano in different tempos, select the tempo that seems "right." Explain why.

19 Dynamics

A CONDUCTOR must be absolutely sure about the meaning of all musical markings. A musical dictionary is a necessary handbook for the student conductor. He must be familiar with all the Italian, German, or French markings that may occur. Many players are confused about them. The mark *pf*, for example, means *poco forte*, a little loud – between *mf* and *f;* not *piano forte*, which would make no sense.

CRESCENDO AND DIMINUENDO

Well-known signs are often misunderstood. A crescendo or diminuendo indicates that growing louder or softer starts where the sign appears. Since Beethoven, the gradual crescendo has become one of the most effective means of building a climax. But the process has to be a gradual one. If a crescendo stretches over thirty-two measures and the orchestra reaches the climax after only sixteen, the tremendous impact of this progressive build-up is lost. For sixteen measures the instruments will try to play still louder; they will overstrain – scratch or blast – and produce hideous tones. Hans von Bülow said, "Crescendo means piano, diminuendo means forte." In a crescendo *save* strength. A corresponding procedure should be used for the diminuendo.

When $<$ $>$ is asked for – covering one or two measures – the crescendo will often be extended too long, with insufficient time for the diminuendo. The climax has to be exactly in the middle (see Chapter 3).

BAROQUE DYNAMICS

The baroque masters seldom used dynamic markings, not because modifications were not made, but because they wrote their works largely for their own use. They *told* their players what kind of dynamics they wanted.

In that period, the time of the harpsichord and organ, there seems to have been little use of a gradual crescendo extending over many measures. Dynamics were more likely to be "terraced," resembling the change of organ registers, which were dynamically stationary.

It has been noted that in the classical period dynamics were the same for all instruments. Trumpets and timpani were accustomed to adapting their tone to the volume of the others. It should be emphasized again (see Chapter 15) that it is up to the conductor to see to it that the important melodic lines emerge clearly, and that instruments apt to predominate (trumpets, trombones) are held in check.

The gradual crescendo, which started in the Mannheim School during the middle of the eighteenth century, paved the way for a more flexible approach. In addition to gradual changes sudden, unexpected shifts in dynamics began to take place.

HAYDN AND MOZART

Haydn favored these sudden contrasts, often for humorous effect. In Mozart's operas there are abrupt shifts as part of the drama. The backstage scream of Zerlina, in *Don Giovanni*, as the Don tries to seduce her, is a notable example. Until this point the three orchestras on stage have been playing light music, for the guests at the party. Then, suddenly, the scream is heard. The stunned guests first listen, then become infuriated, then listen again. There is a constant shift from sharp outbursts to subdued pianos, in the true spirit of musical drama — the kind of drama that no one before Mozart had been able to create.

BEETHOVEN

Beethoven's innate fervor caused him to transfer the drama to his purely orchestral works. He expanded the range of dynamics far beyond the limits of the classical period. His music is full of contrasts, sometimes gradual, sometimes sudden, between massive power and gentleness; he created mysterious tensions by long stretches of "sempre piano," or "sempre *pp*," as in the haunting transition from the scherzo to the finale of his Fifth

Symphony. This "sempre piano" occurs frequently in Beethoven's symphonies, from the finale of his First Symphony on. It may be found in every movement of his Ninth.

Another feature of Beethoven's music is a crescendo that does not end in a climax but breaks off just before. One could call it a "deceptive" climax; it even at times coincides with a deceptive cadence. (In Mozart's operas there are approaches toward similar effects: in *The Marriage of Figaro*, near the end of Cherubino's first aria, and in the last act of *Don Giovanni.*) Examples from Beethoven's works include the first and last movements of the Second Symphony; the first, second, and last movements of the Eroica; and the first and last movements of the Fourth Symphony.

Students might examine additional Beethoven works and identify the places where these sudden pianos are employed.

The performance of a crescendo-piano subito is difficult for a player because of the sudden piano. He must make an abrupt break — like running fast and having to stop suddenly. It is an important effect, however, and conductors must insist on its being done accurately.

Although Haydn favored the sforzato, Mozart made more frequent use of *sfp* (sforzato-piano) and even *fp*. It was for Beethoven's dramatic purposes, however, that the *fp* marking was most valuable. The sudden change heightens the drama. These markings are so frequent in Beethoven's works it would be pointless to list them. Students are directed to the scores.

THE NINETEENTH CENTURY

As the sudden piano after a forte creates a dramatic effect, so does the reverse. Schubert made good use of this effect, as a study of his *Unfinished* Symphony will reveal. The device itself is nothing new. Haydn used it — the most famous example being the "surprise" in his *Surprise* Symphony. All these dynamic contrasts were used more and more frequently and effectively by the nineteenth-century romanticists. The transition from introduction to main allegro in Weber's *Oberon* overture is a good example, as is the first sudden outburst in Mendelssohn's overture to *A Midsummer Night's Dream* and the first forte in the last movement of Brahms's Second Symphony.

In the nineteenth century, not only dynamic contrasts, but the whole dynamic range of the orchestra was greatly extended. The number of instruments increased, the mechanisms of some of them were improved, and players achieved greater technical ability. Tone volume and brilliancy of the orchestra also grew, because of the rise in pitch. (Two hundred years ago it was more than a half step lower than it is today.) A hundred-piece orchestra can play louder than a forty-piece one. And – strangely enough – it can play just as softly, with an even silkier and more velvety tone.*

With the increase in dynamic possibilities composers went to extremes in dynamic markings. Tchaikovsky used *ffff* and even *pppppp* in his *Symphonie Pathétique*. Mahler, in the last movement of his Second Symphony, marks the violins before the entrance of the alto solo *ppppp dim*. These are typically romantic exaggerations. One can scarcely play more softly than *ppp*. At the end of the exposition in the first movement of the *Pathétique* Tchaikovsky writes a *pppp* for the bassoon, in its lowest range, where no player can play more softly than *pp*. Conductors are justified in changing the orchestration by using the much softer bass clarinet in place of the bassoon.

NON-PROFESSIONAL ORCHESTRAS

One of the flaws most frequently found in an untrained orchestra is that it plays with a kind of undefined and unrefined

* Berlioz, in his treatise on orchestration, asks for an orchestra of 21 first violins, 20 seconds, 18 violas, 15 cellos, 10 basses, and a proportionately enlarged wind group: 116 players in all. He says: "Smaller orchestras, even if each player is capable, are ineffective and consequently of little value." Most non-professional orchestras would be glad to have a string section half this size. Fortunately, Berlioz's demand is a romantic overstatement. After all, Beethoven performed his Seventh and Eighth Symphonies with four first violins, four second, two violas, two cellos, and two basses. (This combination was customary in Beethoven's time, though we know today that his imagination had outgrown this undersized orchestra.)

dynamic quality, neither loud nor soft. Of course if a *f* or *ff* is asked for, the orchestra will make a lot of noise. But even in the strongest *ff*, the sound of the brass should always be "golden," not tinny. Strings must never scratch, or woodwinds screech.

A conductor may have even more trouble in getting his group to play a really soft, silky piano passage. Wind players are often members of the school band, where the tone seldom requires the subtlety needed in an orchestra. Among string players, on the other hand, there is a fear of not getting enough "tone" if they are too soft. They should be made to understand that although the soft tone each produces alone may be rather weak and unsubstantial, when they play as a group it may be entirely sufficient. Its lack of substance may create just the right effect. An orchestra will sound much more professional when it can play a passage tenderly and almost inaudibly. The conductor should realize that a well-played *pp* passage makes a more striking impression on a receptive audience than a loud outburst in a *ff*.

As in so many other aspects of music, there are no absolute standards for dynamics. A Mozart forte will be different from one used in a Beethoven or Wagner work (see Chapter 21).

Students should examine many works, chiefly to observe the composers' dynamic demands. They will find that many signs are easily overlooked. When a conductor studies a score for a performance he must carefully study all dynamic marks. There is no excuse for neglecting even the slightest. It is as important to correct faulty dynamics, during a rehearsal, as it is to eliminate incorrect notes.

Some suggestions for studies of dynamics would include Schumann's First and Second Symphonies (the sudden pianos); and the first and last movements of Brahms's First Symphony (in which there are many sudden dynamic changes). All the symphonies of Bruckner, and especially those of Mahler, offer an abundance of dynamic problems. On the other hand, the subtlety of Debussy's dynamics deserves attention. Actually, there are no limits to studies of dynamics, since dynamics are the backbone of music.

20 Phrasing

THE BELIEF that phrasing always complies with bowing marks and slurs is inaccurate. Very often these signs are misleading, and the conductor is forced to apply musicianship to the right phrasing. Markings may often be questionable. Errors may result from a composer's or copyist's negligence.

Phrasing may be compared to speaking, with its inflection, climax, and — when necessary — interruption. A misplaced comma may distort the meaning entirely, as will an improper parenthesis or an exclamation that is not exclamatory. Similarly, the melodic line should be thought of as if it were written for voice. Orchestral musicians often forget this affinity between vocal and instrumental music. It is true that with the development of orchestral music, especially in the works of Wagner, Bruckner, and Strauss, symphonic themes have so expanded that they can no longer be sung in one breath. But this growth is only a matter of degree, since the orchestral apparatus allows much longer melodic lines than the human voice.

PHRASING OF WINDS

The example below is one in which the slurs in wind parts do not coincide with the phrasing. Beethoven's Violin Concerto opens:

The phrasings, indicated by brackets, are in accord with one's natural expectation, but in the original only the bassoons conform to it. In the other winds a slur starts at the beginning of the third measure. Here Beethoven surely did not intend an interruption of the melodic line. His slurrings indicate merely that he wanted the note tongued, with the whole phrase in one breath. That this phrasing complies with Beethoven's intention may be observed in the recapitulation (measure 366). Here the string bowings conform to the suggested phrasing. Woodwinds have the same slurs as at the beginning, but two measures later they, too, match the phrasing. Probably Beethoven felt that a slight taking of breath would be needed because of the forte.

There is a similar problem in the *Nocturne* from Mendelssohn's *Midsummer Night's Dream:* (See ex. 110 on p. 148.) The slurs should be interpreted as in example 110. In the twelfth measure bassoons follow the actual phrasing, but not the solo horn. This piece presents a difficult task for the horn player. An excellent horn is needed because of the extended phrasing. Taking breath after each slur would deprive the work of its musical sense. This is why:

In general, the following rule holds true: When a piece uses upbeat phrases, later phrases will also start on the upbeat.* Applied to Mendelssohn's *Nocturne*, the suggested phrasing becomes self-evident. Thinner brackets show the more subtle inflections of the melody, often at odds with the slurs. Bold brackets indicate full idea. The horn player should take them in one breath. Thin brackets show where breath *may* be taken in emergencies.

* This rule does not apply to large symphonic forms. It does prevail in the minuets and trios of classical symphonies. It is significant that one of the rare exceptions is Mozart's *A Musical Joke,* in which he makes fun of bad musicians. Mozart, the great master of form, here uses an upbeat minuet with a downbeat trio, for him an example of bad musicianship. From Beethoven on, composers shifted the phrase inflection for reasons of contrast. They even changed tempo, as in Beethoven's Seventh Symphony, and meter, as in his *Pastoral* and Ninth. Needless to say, in the later masters (Schumann, Brahms, Bruckner) these contrasting trios occur more frequently.

FOUR

Interpretation

The following example is taken from the second movement of Schubert's *Unfinished* Symphony (see *Workbook*):

This is a very long melodic line (played the first time by a clarinet and the second by an oboe). The first four measures and the following six are slurred. The first phrase ends at the bracket, but Schubert ties the last A (written C for A clarinet) over into the next phrase. He wants no attack at all on the extremely soft F major 6/4 chord. He finishes the slur two measures later, and here a slight breath is justified because of the following accent. Another even less noticeable breath may be taken four measures later, for the very slight accentuation on the G-sharp (B). As the melody fades gradually away additional breath should be unnecessary.

PHRASING AND BOWING

Bowing marks in the strings fail to coincide with the phrasing even more frequently than do slurs in the wind parts. The second movement of Beethoven's Fifth Symphony begins:

The first two measures are balanced by the following two; although the rhythmic pattern is different, this second pair of measures complements the first. After this first phrase, a one-measure pattern occurs with its sequence in the next measure (for variety, the second upbeat is changed from a thirty-second to a sixteenth). A two-measure cadence follows, with the upbeat similar to that in the first measure.

This detailed analysis demonstrates that the bowings do not run parallel to the form. Beethoven, expecting the players to understand the construction, wanted it done as though in one breath. Players should change bows without any noticeable interruption, but the inflection of the melodic line must be made clear by the way it is presented.

This very different example is taken from Johann Strauss's *Tales from the Vienna Woods*:

Ex. 11

No one can think of this phrase differently than marked by our brackets. It is an upbeat melody if there ever was one. If actually phrased as bowed the waltz would lose its Viennese charm – which will be enhanced by the soft and smooth changes of bow.

SHIFTS OF ORCHESTRATION

Very often phrases seem to be interrupted by sudden changes of orchestration. Mozart uses this device, especially in his later symphonies:

In the E-Flat Major Symphony:

First movement (measure 106): the melody shifts from clarinet to flute.

Fourth movement (measure 42 ff.): the theme jumps from strings to woodwinds.

In the G Minor Symphony:

First movement (measure 44): the theme switches from strings to woodwinds and back.

In the *Jupiter* Symphony:

Second movement (measure 19): the upbeat is played by oboe and clarinet, but the melody continues in the strings in the measure following.

From Beethoven on, this device became more and more general. For the sake of variety, with the increasing complexity of form and orchestration, dividing phrases among different instruments was often resorted to.

INTERRUPTED PHRASES

Another kind of shift is to start a new phrase (or phrase section) before the old one has ended. Most often, the last note of one phrase will coincide with the first note of the second. This device appears as early as some of Mozart's symphonies. The minuet of the *Jupiter* starts with a downbeat theme; from measure 24 on, however, a four-measure upbeat passage appears. On its finishing note the downbeat theme returns.

Ex. 114

LONG PHRASES

As early as Bach, phrases and themes appear in instrumental music that extend beyond the limits of the voice. This practice even extends to Bach's vocal music. The first chorus in the *St. Matthew Passion* has a vocal line on one syllable that cannot be sung in one breath. Staggered breathing is necessary. Even some of his solo pieces require a quantity of breath that very few singers can muster. In classical symphonic music phrases are generally simpler and shorter. Nevertheless, starting from the early classical period slow movements sometimes have long phrases which, though subdivided, should be taken "in one breath" in order not to relax the inner tension that carries them along. The following example is from Dittersdorf's *Tournament of Temperaments:*

Ex. 11

The first idea extends up to the double bar. It seems to end on measure 5, but a break here would weaken the tension. The next section is twelve measures long, with the climax on measure 22. After this, the piece ends with a simple cadence, only two measures long.

A very interesting example of an extended melodic line may be found in Haydn's *Farewell* Symphony. This is not one of Haydn's humorous works, in spite of the witty idea that prompted its writing. It is remarkable for its anticipation of romanticism. The following passage from the second movement is charged with constant yearning; only at the end does it become tranquil.

Adagio [not too slow]
[p]
[pp]
[cresc.]
[cresc.]
[f]
[p]
[pp]
[cresc.]
[mf]
[mf]
[cresc.]
[sempre cresc.]
[f]
[p]
[pp]
[p]
etc.
Ex. 116

This melodic line has all the characteristics so peculiar to late (beyond even early) romanticism.

Only a conductor who understands the breadth and sweep of this flight of Haydn's imagination, with its give and take, its tension and resignation, will be able to convey its significance. Added dynamic markings (in brackets) indicate the inflection; in performance they should be used very subtly, if at all.

PHRASING AND CONSTRUCTION

When the conductor has grasped the meaning of the phrasing, first the phrases themselves and then in the context of a whole movement, he is ready to build the movement in his mind in one sweep. He should be able almost to carry a movement from the first note to the last. Then the phrases will fall into their logical places.

The clarity of a construction may be enhanced by the use of proper rubatos (see Chapters 18 and 21). But these rubatos must never be obvious; they should do no more than underline. It is helpful, in this connection, to listen to recordings of one's own conducting since even relatively slight rubatos may be disturbing when heard in playback. An emotion considered appropriate while performing, or at first hearing, may easily sound trite when repeated a few times. Perhaps this is a reason why today's conductors avoid "emotional" tempo changes.

21 Ornaments

CONDUCTORS are often uncertain about the exact meaning of some ornaments, especially those in music before the nineteenth century. That this uncertainty is not limited to performers can be gathered from a quotation from Grove's *Dictionary of Music and Musicians* (1948):

> Earlier writers often wrote the short appogiatura as an eighth or sixteenth note without the stroke, and in many new editions of old compositions we find the small note printed with the stroke even where it should be played long, while in more modern music the sixteenth without the stroke is often met with where the short appogiatura is obviously intended.

For that reason this book will not deal with controversial ornamentation but leave their execution to the musicianship of the conductor; however, he should insist on having all embellishments executed by *every* member of his orchestra exactly as he determines.

Many rules about ornaments, on the other hand, are firmly established. Conductors should be familiar with these principles, especially those concerning *grace notes, trills, shakes,* and *turns.*

There are two kinds of grace notes: appogiaturas and short grace notes.

APPOGIATURAS

Writing an appogiatura in the form of a grace note has been obsolete since the end of the eighteenth century. Today an appogiatura (which is nothing but a suspension) is written as it should be played. In the baroque period the conductor rendered the basic harmonies from the harpsichord; in order to avoid notes foreign to these harmonies, all instruments showed the notes belonging to these chords. Generally, the length of the suspension was indicated by the written value given to the grace note. Therefore the following pattern:  should be played:  and this pattern:  this way:

GRACE NOTES

What we call a grace note today, since the beginning of the nineteenth century the only one in use, was written like the appogiatura but with a line through the stem of the small note.

There has been a controversy as to exactly when the grace note should be played, *before* or *on* the beat. Since Carl Philipp Emanuel Bach defined it, in his treatise on playing the clavier, it has been considered amateurish to play it before the beat. (In the nineteenth century some theorists recommended the latter.) The pattern  generally sounds:

There is a difference of opinion as to which note should be emphasized. Since the two notes follow each other in quick succession, this is not a matter of great significance. The note following the grace note is the more important one, the grace note being nothing more than an added ornament; but the grace note is played *on* the beat, so there is a tendency to accent it rather than the note following it. For this reason emphasis on *both* notes is recommended.

Sometimes two or even three grace notes precede the principal note. They are usually written as sixteenth notes. Although they do not have lines through the stems they are generally short, the speed depending upon the tempo of the piece; in an adagio they are played considerably slower than in an allegro. If played too fast, they may spoil the calm of a slow movement. Not to confuse them with appogiaturas, Mozart usually wrote them as thirty-second or sixty-fourth notes. Beethoven, in the second movement of his Seventh Symphony, writes sixteenth-note grace notes in the counter-theme of the cellos. There is an example of triplet grace notes at the beginning of the Funeral March in the *Eroica* Symphony, in the bass part. It is interesting to note that these grace notes, sounding like a snare drum, appear only during the first three measures of the piece, written as thirty-second grace notes; from then on actual thirty-second notes occur *before* the beat. These triplets become an important thematic element in the work. There is reason to question, therefore, whether Beethoven did not mean the grace notes as well to be played before the beat. In the first movement of Mahler's Third Symphony there is a similar case — and Mahler explicitly asks that they be played before the beat. In Bartok's *Concerto for Orchestra* they are placed before the barline.

Schubert, in the development section of the first movement of the *Unfinished* Symphony, even uses four-note grace notes — besides triplets — as does Bizet, in the farandole of his *L'Arlesienne* suite. These runs on the violin resemble the sound of a whip.

TRILLS (*shakes*)

Different signs have been used for trills. In baroque music the symbols: ∿∿ and ∿∿∿ are to be found, depending upon the number of shakes the composer asked for. Later the familiar "tr" was established, with or without ∿∿∿∿∿ to the end of the trill.

Since Mozart's time, ∿ indicates a simple shake:  . It sounds:  . If there is a line through it: it is a *mordent* and turned downward:  . In German it is called *Pralltriller* ("recoiling trill"). It is sometimes called an "inverted mordent," which is a rather roundabout way of naming such a common ornament. Should the neighboring note have an accidental, it is placed above the sign in a shake (trill) and below in a mordent.

Mozart often used the "tr" sign when he wanted only a simple shake. The pattern:  is to be played  . In slower tempo and if the trill note is a dotted eighth, more than one shake is required.

The following pattern occurs frequently in baroque music, especially at the end of a piece: 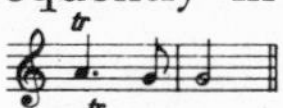 . It should be performed as if it were written:  with the trill ending on the first of the two eighths. However, in this pattern:  the two sixteenths are "after-beats" and the trill continues up to them. (After-beats are also called turns.)

During the baroque period another rule was established. A trill started on the upper note:   . Only if the trill occurred at the beginning of a piece, or if it was preceded by the upper trill note, did the lower note start the trill.

The after-beats mentioned above occur in connection with trills to the present time; they are either written in their actual value, as above, or as grace notes:  .

Composers often do not indicate an after-beat: it is safe to use it if the trill is followed by a note on a heavy beat. When the basic note in a trill is succeeded by the same note, the after-beat will consist of only one note:  . To use an after-beat or not is something each conductor can decide for himself.

TURNS

The symbol for a turn is: . It should be played:  . This shows that the turn starts on the upper note. The following is a turn in slower tempo:  . When a turn occurs between two notes  it is played  . In slower tempo:  . Should the note above the basic note need an accidental it is placed above the turn sign; below the basic note, it is placed below the sign.

If a turn has a line through it, it starts on the lower note. The famous passage from Wagner's *Rienzi* overture:  is done:  . In the slow tempo of the introduction this version is preferable: .

EXAMPLES

It should be stressed that the "right" execution of ornaments is often a matter of personal taste. In one place or another, however, the masters have spelled out what these signs meant to them. This provides at least a conception of how they wanted them done.

The following works contain a variety of ornaments. Some are controversial; suggestions about their execution should lead to interesting discussion.

GLUCK:	Overture to *Iphigenia in Aulis.*
MOZART:	Ballet music *Les petits Riens* (many examples).
	Divertimento No. 15, K. 287 (many examples).
	Linz Symphony, K. 425 (many examples).
	G Minor Symphony, K. 550 (many examples).
	E-Flat Major Symphony, K. 543, second and third movements.
	Prague Symphony, K. 504, first and second movements.
	Flute Concerto in D, K. 314, second movement.
	Flute Concerto in G, K. 313, all movements.
BACH:	*St. Matthew Passion,* last chorus.
	Suite No. 2 in B Minor, introduction.
HANDEL:	Concerto Grosso No. 3 in E Minor, introduction.
	Concerto Grosso No. 2 in F Major, introduction.
	Concerto Grosso No. 11 in A Major, introduction.
	Concerto Grosso No. 5 in G Major, introduction.
HAYDN:	Symphony No. 100 (*Military*), second movement.
	Symphony No. 95 in C Minor, all movements.
	Symphony No. 88 in G Major, Menuetto.
BEETHOVEN:	First Symphony, second movement.

22 *Style*

PLAYING all signs and notes correctly, and grasping the fluctuations of tempo and phrasing, are fundamental to recreation of a masterwork. Having a conception of its style is equally essential. Knowledge of style is the basis of real "interpretation." Some matters of style have been dealt with previously. This chapter provides a compact summary.

The Styles of Different Periods

In baroque music the composer was primarily concerned with construction, less with orchestral color. He employed the instruments available to him and would – in the same work – have used others had they been on hand. Bach knew the colors of the instruments despite these limitations: he is the one composer of his time who should not be tampered with. Handel, on the other hand, changed his instrumentation whenever it suited him. The gradual crescendo was scarcely known and in the middle of the eighteenth century was still regarded as a novelty (see Chapter 19). As to breathing or bowing, there were legato, with phrases in one breath or bow; or non-legato in which the bows were changed on every note and the woodwinds tongued; or interrupted non-legato, martellé, or staccato. When notes are thus placed separately, this staccato is not executed with a "bounce," as was done later with spiccato bowings (see Chapter 11). The sonorous violin tone was developed still later: a fact that applies to most instruments. Bach's Brandenburg Concerto No. 4 – with two recorders, violin, strings, and harpsichord – is difficult to perform today. The violin must use artificial restraint to avoid drowning out the other solo instruments.

In the time of the rococo, the gallant age, a lighter tone production developed. The staccato was used more frequently and was done spiccato. This style coincides with the advent of the classical symphony.

During the romantic period the individual styles of the composers became more and more pronounced. There were great differences among the early romantics – Schumann, Mendelssohn,

Liszt, Chopin. There were equally great differences among the later ones – Brahms, Wagner, Verdi, Tchaikovsky; and the latest – Richard Strauss, Mahler, and Debussy. All through romanticism the emphasis was on emotion and drama. The first reaction occurred with the advent of impressionism's subtle airiness.

The twentieth century has seen the development of many different styles, from expressionism to neo-classicism, from atonality to primitivism, from post-romanticism to electronic music. It may be said that a reaction against the highly emotional style of late romanticism has taken place. Much contemporary music should be performed with the technique of the early eighteenth century.

National Styles

The national character of a piece will often provide a clue to its style. Latin music – Spanish, Italian, French – has a spirit of its own. Spanish music reflects the stateliness, pride, and strong rhythmic sense of the Spaniards. Italian music is highly spirited, emphasizing melody (*bel canto*), which comes so easily to the people whose language is most singable of all. In French music there is a combination of both but the greater subtlety of the French *esprit* prevails. There is transparency, delicacy, refinement. There are strong dramatic sections, but in Italian music climaxes are elementary whereas the French drama is more calculated.

In the nineteenth century the sudden emergence of Russian music was one of the most striking developments. Typically Slavic characteristics prevail: Eastern folklore (often with an oriental timbre), emotional outbursts, passages of melancholy, are presented in sparkling orchestral color.

American music plays an important part in the emergence of new trends. Jazz and American folklore give this music a special style. For effective performance utmost rhythmic precision and sharpness are needed.

Personal Styles

There is a clear difference between the styles of Bach and Handel, but the approach to their orchestral music – as to all music of the baroque period, from the technical point of view – must be very similar.

In the classical period, Haydn's style may be called highly diversified. He has a great sense of humor, but drama and even melancholy enter his music. The emotional range of his 104 symphonies is amazing in its breadth. Nevertheless he is simpler, earthier, less sophisticated than Mozart, in whose music can be found an anticipation of the romantic period.

Performing Mozart needs a greater refinement of style than is required for practically any other master.

Next comes Beethoven, a master who stubbornly adheres to his own ideal; a giant, not to be measured by traditional standards. He found new ways to use orchestral color, but the orchestra remains a means to express musical ideas and to delineate musical construction. Accents, surprising break-offs after an accumulation of tension, are abundant in his work. The harsh *fp*'s, the shock of a sudden piano after a crescendo, should not be smoothed: these are inherent characteristics of his style.

Schubert may be called a classical romanticist. His style is subdued. Romanticism is expressed in the lovely melodies in the instrumental works of this great Austrian song composer. Even secondary voices can "sing" their parts.

Berlioz was the first to emphasize orchestral color (he even wrote a treatise about it), but Schubert, Weber, and then Mendelssohn had all used the orchestral palette with a sensitivity not known up to their time. Mendelssohn, too, is classical in his romanticism. But it is more derived from literature, with a fairy-tale touch. Emotions are subtle. Outbursts and powerful climaxes are rare. The sprightly and elflike character of his music requires a technically well-schooled orchestra.

Schumann is one of the great masters of romantic emotion, although he is not primarily an orchestral composer. A good conductor should have no difficulty in grasping his ideas, but because of a lack of brilliance in the orchestration he will need a competent orchestra when it comes to making them sound convincing.

Brahms knew well how to write for orchestra, but his texture is not easy to comprehend. Phrasing, cross rhythms, and the interplay of voice lines cause difficulties to non-professionals. Wagner, though technically more intricate than Brahms, is easier to perform because of his brilliant orchestration. Every player can "enjoy" working on his part.

Among the Russian composers Tchaikovsky is the most popular. He has a very colorful orchestral style, but difficult passages for most instruments. If these can be mastered technically there will be few problems in performance, since his style is so obviously emotional.

The sublety of the French impressionists (Debussy, Ravel) was a clear reaction to the massive power of the Germanic Wagner style.

Different Styles in the Work of the Same Composer

Although a conductor may be aware of a composer's individual style, he also has to recognize within the master's work varieties of character and weight. This requires a variety of ways of playing legatos, staccatos, or whatever the case may be. March and dance-like pieces, for example, need lightness, sprightliness, and emphasis on rhythm. Notes should be played short even without staccato marks. In classical music this applies principally to the minuet and the scherzo. Waltzes seldom use staccato markings; no one should play the typical [musical notation] of a waltz as [musical notation] (see Chapter 11).

It is interesting to observe how the masters dealt with these problems. In their original scores Haydn and Mozart often failed to use staccato signs for short notes. When they wanted to make it very clear that quarter or eighth notes should be played staccato they did add the marks, Haydn more often than Mozart.

The latter took it for granted that a good musician would understand the style.

Even first and last movements of symphonies may at times require the lighter touch. Here staccatos are marked when *especially* short notes are wanted. In Mozart's G Minor Symphony the first theme is written:

Ex. 117a

Of course it should be played:

Allegro molto

Ex. 117b

but with a light tone, not an actual staccato.

The beginning of Mozart's *Haffner* Symphony is interesting: Mozart marks some quarter notes staccato. Others should be *almost* as short, if not quite so crisp. This may sound contradictory to what has been previously recommended (see Chapter 17), that is, to give each note its full value unless marked otherwise. It is not. Besides being accurate, the conductor needs a sense of style if he is to train his group to understand the subtleties of good playing.

Another aspect often neglected is the difference between staccatos in fast and slow movements. Sometimes a staccato note in a slow movement should be held longer than a non-staccato in a fast movement. In the second movement of Beethoven's Fifth Symphony the first staccato note, if done very short, would sound like a rather silly kick-off. There has to be a certain elegance in the way this note is played; it should be light, but not cut off like a staccato in a scherzo. (Ex. 112.)

There is a similar situation at the beginning of the slow movement of Beethoven's First Symphony (see *Workbook*).

Sometimes, in a slow movement, a composer asks for a stilted or humorous style. In such cases short staccatos are indicated. This occurs in the famous andante of Haydn's *Surprise* Symphony.

In the "clock" movement of his *Clock* Symphony, the "tick-tock" should naturally be as crisp as possible. Haydn not only places dots over the notes but adds the word "staccato"; he wants to make it absolutely clear.

There are many varieties of style in music; as a topic it is practically inexhaustible. No foolproof recipe can be given to a prospective conductor. These few directions should induce him to scrutinize with a searching mind and a keen sense of musicianship the work he wants to perform – not to mention a knowledge of the place in history each master occupies and of his very special characteristics.

Practical Matters FIVE

23 *Seating*

ACOUSTICS

THE BEST way to seat an orchestra has always been a matter of controversy. Today some arrangements have become standard. However – and this is the strongest argument against standard seating – much depends upon the acoustics of the hall and especially of the stage or orchestra pit. The quality of the orchestra, its size, and the proportion of strings to winds also play major parts in determining the seating.

One fact has to be borne in mind: The conductor hears those instruments best that play close to him. Usually the weaker string players sit further away, where their shortcomings will be less noticeable to him; therefore he must keep a keen eye – and ear – on them. It is advisable to make tape recordings during rehearsals. They will show unmercifully the shortcomings of both the acoustics and the players, and will disclose mistakes that the conductor was not able to hear from the podium. These recordings have to be made with good equipment by experienced technicians; a second-rate playback may do more harm than good. The microphone must be placed correctly, and the recording sound should be as faithful as possible. What the conductor may hear, if the sound is distorted, can sometimes be disheartening enough to make him abandon hope. The musicians too should listen to these playbacks, in order to become aware of their shortcomings.

What constitutes the acoustically best seating is often a matter of opinion. Frequently one's hearing is influenced by preconceived ideas about what *ought* to sound best. The matter is further complicated by the fact that no orchestra will play a passage exactly the same way each time.

STRINGS

Practical Matters

It is an established custom to seat the strings closest to the conductor, with the first violins at his left. The set-up of the other strings varies. Formerly the second violins sat at his right, but during this century the violas or cellos were placed there. One reason for the change is that since the late romantic era viola parts have become more independent and important. Another is that since the first and second violins often play similar passages closer contact seems called for. As a result, the second violins were seated next to the first. The violas were seated on the outside, to the right of the conductor. In classical music, however, violas and second violins often share the middle voices with similar patterns. If they were separated by the cellos this unity might be disturbed. Many conductors consequently place the cellos at their right. This seating has another advantage: with the first violins on the left, followed by the seconds, the violas next, and the cellos right (basses stand behind the cellos) the strings are arranged from top to bottom around the conductor.

Even when the stage is large the group should not be spread. Players should sit as close to one another as possible, with elbow room for each musican but no more. This is of special importance for non-professional groups. Players must learn to listen to one another. Scattered seating makes this difficult.

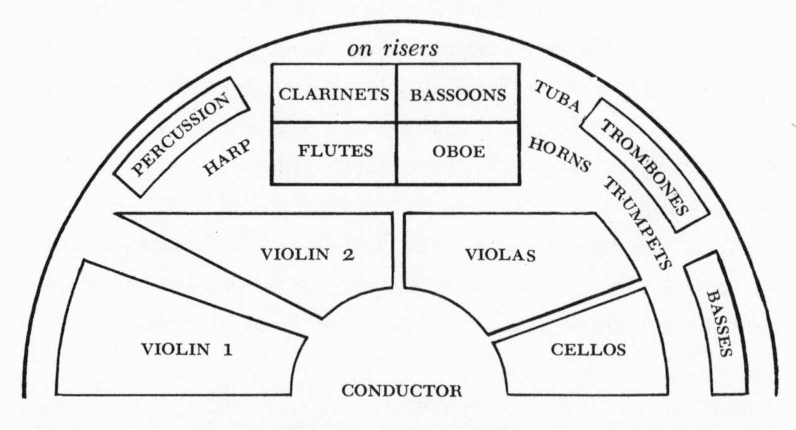

ORCHESTRA SEATING CHART

WOODWINDS AND BRASS

Woodwinds are best located in the center, behind the strings; flutes and oboes in front, clarinets and bassoons behind (or exchange oboes and clarinets). First players should be seated in the center; first flute next to first oboe, first clarinet next to first bassoon. Bassoons and cellos should be close. Brass and percussion may then be placed, at the discretion of the conductor, on both sides of the woodwinds. These are flexible suggestions, depending on acoustics.

SPECIAL PROBLEMS

If the hall has a curtained stage, the sound may be improved by placing the strings as far out as possible on the apron (the arched space in front of the curtain). Some theaters produce exactly the opposite phenomenon. When the strings are outside the curtain line, they sound dull.

On the stage itself there may be diverse situations. If the stage is large, a cyclorama could be used to fill in the space between the orchestra and the rear wall. Depending upon its material the cyclorama may absorb or reflect sound. If the orchestra is weak an absorbent one would be out of place; then a transportable plywood shell could be a solution. This gives rise to a new danger: if the brass sits too close to the reflecting wood its sound may be amplified – especially the horns, since their bells face backward.*

If the orchestra has insufficient strings, seat the brass in a spot that tends to reduce their sound; placed on the side, for example, they will play into the wings rather than the audience. They should get used to keeping their bells low, where the clothing of the other players will help to absorb the blare. (Some trumpet players have a habit of raising their bells, as if they were always playing fanfares.)

* It may happen that seating the horns any place possible still has them predominate in classical music. This may occur especially if the orchestra plays recordings. A good solution is to have them use their overcoats and hang them on the back of a chair directly behind the bells.

If there is a great lack of strings, it is better to seat all the available ones at the left of the conductor. The woodwinds would then be placed at the right. This arrangement is generally used in theaters.

An orchestra pit creates new problems; it is narrow in depth and extended in width. Each group — strings, winds, etc. — should therefore sit together.* But even the best seating arrangement will not prevent the orchestra from drowning out the singers if the conductor fails to adjust the balance (see Chapters 6 and 27).

CHORAL WORKS

When conducting a work for chorus and orchestra, with or without soloists, the conductor faces an especially hard problem. It is one that seems to have caused trouble for many choral societies. Some of the charts for performances in the eighteenth and nineteenth centuries still exist. From them it is evident that it seemed more important to hear the chorus clearly than the orchestra. The chorus was not placed behind the orchestra as is usually done today. A chorus standing before the orchestra would prevent the conductor from being seen by the musicians so the chorus was placed at both sides of the players. This, however, impeded the unity of the choral group. Many of the nineteenth-century charts show an arrangement that, though a compromise, provides a solution. The chorus is placed on both sides of the conductor, leaving only enough space for him to stand between and still be close to the orchestra. It has the disadvantage that the chorus must stand at an angle to the audience when watching the conductor; with some training, however, it should be possible for the chorus to face the audience while keeping the corner of its eye on the conductor.

* It may sometimes be advisable in a theater to seat the strings against the back wall of the pit, while woodwinds and brass sit on the sides. The wall reflects the strings. With the usual seating, the strings may be too weak.

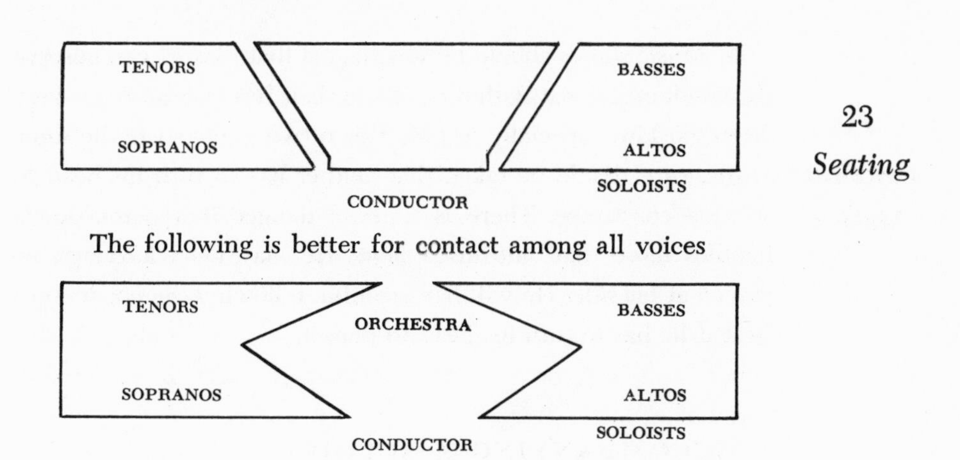

If the choral performance takes place in a theater, best results will be obtained by putting the orchestra in the pit. This is an arrangement similar to opera but better, since the singers will remain constantly at the most advantageous place on the stage. (Choruses should preferably stand on risers; singers in the back will be heard better.) If the chorus is very strong and the acoustics of the hall allow this, it may be placed on risers rather high up behind the orchestra if both are on stage.

SEEING THE CONDUCTOR

One of the most important rules for any kind of performance, choral, orchestral, or both, is that everyone must have a clear view of the conductor. The singers should, preferably, know their music from memory. If they use parts, they should hold them low enough not to impede the free flow of the tone and to keep their eyes on the conductor. Parts should be used only for quick glances, preferably during rests. Each singer should have his own part.

Orchestra members always play from parts but their eyes need not be glued to them. Laymen often wonder how a musician is able to follow a conductor's beat while reading his music. Actually, the human eye is constructed so that seeing at an angle is not difficult; but this angle should be kept as narrow as possible. Music stands should be so adjusted that players can observe the conductor's beat without shifting their heads. Stands are very often too low, especially in pits. When two players use the same music, care should be taken that neither has to turn his head to see the conductor. There is especial danger if a percussionist handles more than one instrument. He may need a xylophone placed at his side. He will have trouble following the conductor's beat if he has to turn his head to play it.

ACCOMPANYING A SOLOIST

When accompanying an instrumental soloist with his orchestra, the conductor should be as close to him as possible in order to observe every detail of his playing. For a piano concerto it is best to have the instrument placed in the middle of the stage. The conductor should stand slightly raised behind the piano, in the center of the stage facing half left.

LIGHTING

Conductors and players should have their music well lighted — not, however, to the point that either is almost blinded. It should be kept in mind that the paper of a conductor's score reflects light, and that when he conducts without a score he is less conspicuous to the players. (For lighting the pit for opera performances, see Chapter 27.)

24

Rehearsals

Discipline

AN ORCHESTRA should become accustomed to the strictest discipline. The conductor may be sincerely gentle and warm-hearted as a man, but when he rehearses he must become autocratic. His job is to draw the best from his players and achieve a performance as close as possible to the ideal. This does not mean, however, that he should abuse the orchestra, insult the players, or imitate a tyrant. Some of the great conductors are known to have been unduly harsh with their orchestras, but these methods are not to be imitated by young conductors.

The conductor's behavior will depend largely upon his temperament. A high-strung conductor may sometimes become excited at rehearsals, but he should never lose control. He may raise his voice to arouse the orchestra, but he must never sound ridiculous and induce laughter. The orchestra will be more attentive when the conductor gives his instructions in an ordinary, almost soft voice, if his corrections are to the point and authoritative. When his players realize that his criticisms are impersonal and intended only for improving performance they will not resent being corrected. Some players, however, will be more sensitive than others and unable to take criticism without feeling hurt personally. The less mature or secure they are, the more often this will happen. A conductor who applies a little psychology will, after a few rehearsals, be able to judge which players will improve by harsh and which by kindly treatment.

One of the first requirements for a disciplined orchestra is that rehearsals start on time. In schools and colleges, students are often late through no fault of their own. These delays are unfortunate. They spoil the morale of the orchestra. It may be a good idea to schedule rehearsals after classes.

Tuning up

The rehearsal should not start before every instrument has tuned up. Players generally need warming-up time – though not so much as is often used – and preferably this should be done outside the actual rehearsal area. As soon as a musician has taken his seat his first task is to tune up. The oboe gives the A, over and over, until all instruments are adjusted. If there is no oboe, a tuning pipe may be advisable or an electrical device, (*i.e.*, a stroboconn); sometimes a reliable trumpet player may give the A. All instruments should tune up as softly as possible (see Chapter 9). No scratching or blasting should be permitted; it dulls musical sensitivity, and if players cannot hear themselves they will not get the right pitch. For string players less than half the bow is sufficient. Woodwinds can tune softly in the middle register, while it is good for the brass to get used to soft playing from the beginning.

Delegate responsibility by having the leader of each group supervise the tuning of his section. In an advanced group the concertmaster should be responsible for tuning, with the conductor entering the rehearsal area only after this has been done. This is the only acceptable method for concerts; if extended to rehearsals it would be ideal. Unfortunately, for tuning up, the average non-professional orchestra needs the supervision of the conductor.

The conductor should not allow players to leave the rehearsal area without his permission, even when they are not needed, because there are always delays in getting them back. All players, even those who have rests, should sit straight in their chairs. A slouchy posture makes it impossible to play precisely and vigorously — or softly and sensitively.

Rehearsals should last longer, if possible, than the usual class hour of fifty minutes. The latter is insufficient when one considers the amount of time needed for warming up, tuning up, and getting the "feel" of the music. Professional orchestras have at least two and a half hours of rehearsal time; an hour and a quarter for non-professionals would be adequate. No intermission is necessary. Rehearsals of more than ninety minutes should have a ten- or fifteen-minute break; but if the set time is not adhered to strictly ten minutes will become fifteen, fifteen become twenty or more. These seemingly small details are important. It pays to avoid lapses in discipline, even in secondary matters.

THE START

There are several ways to start the rehearsal, depending largely upon the quality of the group. It is best to play a major part of a piece without stopping, so the players may get some enjoyment and stimulation from the music itself. There should be no difference in devotion to the task, between rehearsal and concert; even if the rehearsal is at the end of the day, and the players feel tired, it is no excuse for careless, inattentive playing. A stimulating conductor can make an orchestra recover quickly from any kind of weariness.

Another good way to start is with fifteen or twenty minutes of sight reading, counted from the exact moment the rehearsal should start. Pieces should be selected that lie within the players' ability. Young players love trying new works; they frequently are bored with doing the same piece over and over again. If they know that sight reading is reserved only for the beginning of rehearsals it may encourage them to come on time. Of course, "sight reading" only applies to the orchestra. The conductor must be thoroughly familiar with the work if the players are to get any benefit from it. Giving cues will be especially necessary. The tempo has to be "right"; that is, not too fast for the orchestra to follow, not so slow that there is an absence of musical sense. Sight reading should be suspended a few weeks before a performance; all efforts must then be concentrated on the program.

Quality

There is — and this should be borne in mind by any young conductor — a great divergence of view between what a competent leader feels is a good performance and what the average players think is sufficient. How often will the conductor hear: "It will be all right at the concert." Unfortunately, if high standards do not prevail, the concert usually is what they believe to be "all right." But when the players' families and friends attend the concert, and it sounds even passable, their reception will be enthusiastic. The family will be proud that their offspring plays in a group that sounds almost like a real orchestra. The young conductor may have suffered during the performance because of its shortcomings, but he will have difficulty convincing his group that it would have done better had it played more accurately.

More often than not he will even keep silent so as not to discourage his young players. However, nothing succeeds like success. With the necessary discipline and spirit he can achieve better results with better rehearsals. If he has relentlessly trained his group in a work they can do he may yet accomplish astonishing performances. He can make his players do a better job than they themselves thought possible and when they recognize that, they will follow him on the way to greater perfection.

PROBLEMS

The conductor must use his rehearsal time to best advantage. He may sometimes have to discuss a problem with one section while the others are forced to wait. Idle players are apt to be restless – or "eager beavers" will choose this time to go over difficult passages for themselves. The conductor must insist there be absolute silence whenever he stops the orchestra for the purpose of giving instructions.

Some members of the group may tend to continue to play after the conductor has stopped the orchestra. They want to finish the passage they are playing. The conductor should insist on strict discipline; this habit is time-consuming, and very often the passage the conductor wishes to correct is no longer fresh in the ears of the orchestra. All members should be taught to stop at the exact moment the conductor gives the signal.

Time-Saving Devices

REHEARSAL LETTERS

When the conductor stops the orchestra because of an error, he should give an exact and clear explanation of what was wrong and show – preferably by singing – how he wants it done. No time should be lost finding the spot in question.

Orchestral parts have what are called rehearsal letters or numbers; in some editions all measures are numbered, permitting the conductor to call for any measure. When there are letters they are often far apart, and some counting will be needed. The conductor should not, however, count the measures alone, then say to the orchestra, "Eighteen measures before C." Time will be saved by saying "Before C," waiting until everybody has the C, then counting loudly, "one, two, three," up to eighteen. The entire orchestra should join in counting and, when reaching eighteen, everyone should be ready to play.

Since letters are often far apart further letters may be added, especially when a difficult passage is far from a letter. At the beginning of such passages "A/1," "B/1," etc., should be inserted.

INTERRUPTIONS

It would be unreasonable to stop the orchestra every time a flaw appears. For the fastidious conductor there is practically no measure that could not be improved in some way; but, he should attend to matters gradually, starting with the most flagrant mistakes and coming to the subtle ones as time goes on. When an instrument or group has lost its place there is no choice but to stop. Stopping at other times, however, when young players are beginning to feel some inspiration from the sound, the emotion, and the beauty of the work, can be a frustrating experience. They are unable to judge shortcomings from the conductor's perspective. Still worse, imagine the feelings of, say, a trombone player who has forty-five measures rest, has counted diligently up to forty-one, and then has to stop. He must start counting again, and without having had the enjoyment of playing. Young players are bound to get restless. The conductor must make it quite clear that he does not stop for petty reasons and that he, too, would be glad to play the piece through, but that he has no choice. At such moments eagerness to do a good job and respect for the conductor must be heavily relied upon.

MARKING

It is most important that each player *always* have a pencil with which to mark his part as the conductor directs. These marks may concern bowings, fingerings, tonguing by the winds, neglected sudden pianos, gradual crescendos, and similar matters. The player should make additions or very clearly circle marks he overlooked. In any professional orchestra this procedure is common usage, but a student will often insist that he has "a good memory." He must learn from the beginning that a pencil is almost as vital as his instrument. Nothing is so annoying as having to correct the same mistake over and over again.

Much time can be saved if bowings and fingerings are marked in all parts. The conductor should carefully mark the full score. For this he may acquire the assistance of members of the different sections. Then, each individual part should be marked. If it is necessary to add rehearsal numbers or letters, this too can be done before rehearsals.*

SECTION REHEARSALS

One of the best ways to save time is to organize section rehearsals — which may sometimes be more valuable than full rehearsals. Which combinations should be chosen depends upon the quality of the players; in some instances all strings, all woodwinds, and all brasses (with percussion) may be sufficient. At other times it may be better to rehearse each string group separately. The weaker the group, the more section rehearsals it will need. These should not exceed an hour; sometimes a half hour may be enough. The conductor should sit at the piano and softly play the missing instruments from the score. (It is essential for a conductor to become more and more proficient at score

* A very important job in any orchestra is that of a good librarian. One person may not suffice for this job, depending upon the time he can spend. It is not an assignment to be handled in a few minutes before and after rehearsal; if this is tried, the library will deteriorate. The librarian may also be asked to assist the conductor in such matters as marking parts.

playing at the piano.) Section rehearsals for amateur orchestras are not quite so easy to arrange as in student groups.

As soon as a conductor has brought his orchestra to a certain level of quality, as soon as it is capable of playing a piece without any major errors, he should focus his attention on minor flaws. He should devote a full rehearsal to them. His players will be thrilled at the following rehearsal, when they play the entire piece and discover they sound more professional. The conductor should study his score before the rehearsal and mark the weak spots that need practicing. The first may be on page 10; he should mark "10" on the very first page. On page 10 a short remark will indicate what needs improvement. He will then discuss it with his group and play it. The passage in question may end on page 14. The next flaw is on page 29; he should write "29" on page 14, and so on. By doing this much time will be saved. The orchestra will realize that it is not playing the whole piece again and again, but working on necessary improvements.

In conclusion, set the highest possible standards of performance as the goal. For this purpose insist on strictest discipline, but have patience and a sense of humor, and never let time be wasted by inefficient rehearsal practices.

25 *Conducting from memory*

MOST professional conductors today do not use scores at concerts. An aspiring conductor, consequently, believes it a "must" to direct from memory although quite often he is not *thoroughly* acquainted with the music. It is true that if the orchestra is competent and he knows where meter and tempo changes occur and where he has to give necessary cues, there is little danger that anything untoward will happen. Nevertheless a conductor who does not have the score clearly in his head has no business conducting without one. A beginner will probably not be able to write the score from memory, note for note — but he must be skilled enough to think the whole score through in his mind, from the first measure to the last.

It is not advisable to conduct a non-professional orchestra from memory. Should something go wrong in a secondary part the conductor without a score would need extraordinary ability to straighten matters out. Even when there is no obvious mistake, but a passage is not played to the conductor's liking, it may be enough to divert his mind. In sum he should know the score from memory but use the score in performance. (When a conductor has memorized the score and has it in front of him, it will, strangely enough, assist him in moments of distraction even if he does not actually look at it. Again it is the corner of the eye that does the job.)

A conductor's eyes are one of his most important tools. They can sometimes be more stimulating, more expressive, than any manual gesture. They should not be buried in the score. This is another reason for the conductor to have the music in his head.

As part of his training every student conductor ought to be required to conduct from memory, at rehearsal, a piece of about ten minutes' length. It would furnish proof that he has studied the score thoroughly as well as help him to master any other score.

MEMORIZING

The technique of memorizing depends largely on individual faculties of retention. One student may have what is called a "photographic" memory, and may be able to visualize the score. Another may retain the melodic and structural basis of a work faster than details, whereas a third may have a strong sense of its harmonic organization. These differing faculties furnish a starting point. Then details have to be considered — the exact arrangement of the voices, the entrances of secondary parts, the subtleties of dynamics, exact note values.

A conductor, even if he has not a "photographic" memory, should not use two differently arranged scores, keeping one for rehearsals and another, perhaps a pocket edition, for memorization and home study. It renders retention more difficult when a particular passage may be on the right hand page, end of the line, in one score, but on the left hand page, beginning of the line, in another. The orchestra seating arrangement should also remain the same, at all rehearsals and at concerts. If there is a change in the direction in which the conductor must give cues, and from which he hears the different instruments of the orchestra, it will add another burden to his capacity for retention.

In conclusion, it should become a young conductor's practice to memorize his scores, even though he would be wise to use them in a performance.

Additional Conducting Skills

SIX

26 Choral conducting

THERE is a mistaken notion that different kinds of beats are used for conducting an orchestra and conducting a chorus. Actually the difference is not in baton technique but areas of knowledge. For orchestra conducting one has to understand the function of the instruments, whereas for leading a chorus one has to know the technical problems of the human voice, diction, and the like. There should be no difference in the beat. Young choral conductors often believe they must acquire some special choral conducting technique; with musicianship, a good ear, and knowledge of vocal problems, even without the right technique, they may even achieve good vocal results. There is one more danger connected with so-called choral technique. The leader molds vocal phrases: after each one he gives the singers time to take breath. This lack of a steady beat disturbs the regularity and order of the meter.

A problem arises when the ambitions of the choral group grow. Having done *a capella* work and choruses with piano accompaniment, the choir may want to attempt a work with orchestra. Instrumentalists have trouble, however, with conductors who have their own peculiar "choral" beat. The chorus, having studied diligently, may do a good job even while the orchestra is being confused by the unorthodox beat. The chorus will be forced, haphazardly, to follow its concertmaster in order to remain together. Had the chorus leader learned the general rules of conducting the confusion would never have arisen.

Except for the chapters on the instruments, there is nothing in this book that should not be useful to a prospective choral conductor. The chapters on instruments can in fact provide him information for the day he decides to conduct an orchestra with his chorus. Suggestions made in the chapters on accompaniment (Chapter 28) and opera conducting (Chapter 29) should be of additional help.

The first exercises of this book were vocal, partly because every student carries his voice with him, partly because all instrumental conducting should be based on the rules of good singing. This too underlines the affinity between vocal and orchestral performing.

SEATING

There are at present different points of view about seating (or rather standing) of the chorus. The conservative idea is to place each group separately, sopranos left of the conductor, altos right, tenors behind altos and basses behind sopranos, or tenors and basses interchanged. Were tenors behind sopranos, the higher female and male voices would stand together; by placing tenors behind altos, voices closest in range are placed together.

The other school of thought strives for the perfect blend. It is a new idea – a combination of all voices, with sopranos, altos, tenors, basses mixed together. This is, of course, an added strain on the individual singer, because being surrounded by voices singing the same part adds security. The mixed position requires much more thorough rehearsal (during rehearsal the voice parts stand together until they are entirely familiar with the music) because each singer must depend entirely upon himself. But it can be done, and many chorus directors are proud of having a trained group and a perfectly unified blend.

For homophonic music this idea may have its advantages. Matters are different in polyphonic works. The entrances of the different voices afford a special fascination by coming from different directions. Stereophonic recordings are based on this concept. The work becomes more "plastic." Mixing the voices would destroy this structural impression; nobody would ever suggest mingling string players with woodwinds, brass, or percussion, but the idea is the same. The traditional chorus arrangement is therefore recommended.

CHORUS AND ORCHESTRA

All schools and colleges have choruses and bands, and most have orchestras. It is regrettable that they seldom combine forces. Many stirring works for chorus and orchestra (or band) deserve performance. One thinks, almost inevitably, of Handel's *Messiah,* part of which seems to be constantly on the programs of professional and non-professional groups. The *Messiah,* of course, is one of the greatest masterworks, and it is not difficult to perform it (or parts of it) creditably. The *Hallelujah* chorus, especially, may be sung by any trained school group; it will stir singers and orchestra alike and will almost always receive an enthusiastic response from the audience. Other sections of the *Messiah* are more difficult. Still, compare it with other famous masterworks: Bach's B Minor Mass and *St. Matthew Passion,* Haydn's *Creation,* Beethoven's *Missa Solemnis,* Mendelssohn's *Elijah,* Mozart's *Requiem,* Verdi's *Requiem,* Brahms's *German Requiem.* The *Messiah* is, for chorus as well as orchestra, within the scope of any good non-professional group.

It is also true, however, that the *Messiah* is frequently performed by great professional choruses and orchestras. There are several first-rate performances on records. This raises one of the most basic issues in music education: whether it is more important to stir students' enthusiasm with unprofessional renditions of masterworks, or to start with works — maybe not so sublime — that are more within their scope. The latter approach is recommended.

BAROQUE

There are a large number of excellent works by baroque (and later) masters that are much easier to perform than any of the great masterworks. These compositions can give the chorus, the orchestra, and the audience a great deal of satisfaction.*

A good start may be made with works by Heinrich Schütz, the great German master who was born a hundred years before Bach and Handel. Very suitable is his *Seven Last Words of Christ* (AMP, Bä.). There are also the *Our Father* (Br.); *Magnificat* (AMP); *Christmas Oratorio* (AMP, Pe.); three *Passions* (all AMP); and *136th Psalm* (Bä.). In the same era Monteverdi wrote his great operas. His *Scherzi Musicali* (two vol., Bä.) are charming works written for three vocal parts and strings, which may be performed with single voices or chorus (not too large). Toward the end of the seventeenth century Buxtehude was one of the great masters. (Bach traveled more than a hundred miles on foot to study with him.) His works are much simpler than Bach's and lend themselves well to student performance. (Bä., Br.)

One of the earliest available musical works, combining vocal and instrumental music, is a piece called *London Street Cries* (AMP) by Orlando Gibbons. There are several works by Henry Purcell, the great English master of the seventeenth century, in the same catalogue. He also composed a fine *Te Deum* (Sch.). Additional choral works with orchestra suitable for non-professional organizations are compositions by Caldara (L.), Scarlatti (L., AMP), Sammartini (Pe.), Telemann (Bä.), Lully (AMP), and, especially, Vivaldi's *Gloria* (Sch., Colombo).

Handel wrote a number of unduly neglected smaller works.

* The following compilation of these works lists publishers, using the following abbreviations: Associated Music Publishers: AMP; Bärenreiter (Kassel, Germany): Bä.; Boosey and Hawkes: Bo.; Broude Brothers: Br.; Carl Fischer: F.; Edwin F. Kalmus: Ka.; Leeds Music: L.; Peters Edition: Pe.; G. Schirmer: Sch. Works are recommended for which choral and orchestral parts can be obtained. In many cases orchestral parts may be purchased only from Edwin F. Kalmus. Some orchestrations have been reproduced from old copies and may be difficult to decipher, but they are often the only parts available. The conductor or his assistant may have to retouch some parts in order to make them understandable to his players. Most of these works can be rented from the Mapleson Music Library, 129 West 29th Street, New York 1, N.Y. Some works are only obtainable on a rental basis from the original publisher.

Some listed below have great charm, others reflect the power and grandeur of his masterful oratorios.

Psalm 96 (Pe.).
Psalm 112 (Pe.).
Dettingen Te Deum (Pe.).
Utrecht Te Deum (Pe.).
Hymn, *O Praise the Lord* (AMP).
Ode to St. Cecilia's Day (Ka.). Almost as long as an oratorio, but simpler and very charming.
Funeral anthem, *On the Death of Queen Caroline* (Br.).
Donna Che in Ciel (L.).

One of Handel's first choral works is his *St. John Passion* (Pe.). It, too, is simpler in style than his later masterworks.

Bach wrote hundreds of cantatas, many of which should be within the capacity of student groups (AMP, Ka.) The conductor should study the scores of these cantatas to find which ones lend themselves best to his purpose. In many cantatas vocal soloists are used in addition to the chorus. The conductor will know which kinds of soloists are at his disposal, and make his choices accordingly. Many have difficult instrumental solo passages.

LATER WORKS

Since this book does not specialize in choral music it can provide only a limited number of suggestions from the abundance of music for chorus and orchestra. The following is a list of classical, romantic, and some contemporary compositions that deserve to be performed.

HAYDN:
Theresa Mass (Br.).
Nelson Mass (Sch.).
Seven Last Words of Christ (Sch.).

The Seasons (AMP) is of course a full length oratorio, but it is not performed as often as it should be, being overshadowed by the master's great *Creation*. It has a refreshing näiveté and charm; the soloists should be of professional standard. Since most of the choruses are within the scope of non-professional organizations, it may be valuable to perform at least parts of this masterwork.

MOZART:	*Missa Brevis,* K. 258 (AMP).
	Coronation Mass (AMP, Sch.).
	Regina Coeli (AMP, Sch.).
	Kyrie in D Minor (Sch.). A short work, worth performing.
	Misericordias Domini (Sch.). An early work, remarkable for its contrapuntal skill, not too difficult.
	Mass in C Minor (AMP). A masterwork, not easy.
	Ave Verum Corpus (AMP). One of Mozart's sublime works, often performed, but seldom with orchestra (strings).
	Litany in E-Flat Major (AMP). A fine work, two soloists needed, but not too difficult.
	Santa Maria (Br.). Not difficult.
	Te Deum (Br.). Not difficult.
	Vespers, K. 339, (AMP).
	Freemason Cantata, K. 429, (AMP).
BEETHOVEN:	Mass in C (AMP, Br.). Not so demanding as his *Missa Solemnis,* not an easy work, worth performing.
SCHUBERT:	Turn Your Thoughts, from *Lazarus* (Br.).
	Mass in C. (Sch.).
	Mass in F (Sch.).
	Mass in G (AMP, Ka.).
	Mass in A-Flat (AMP, Pe.).
	Mass in E-Flat (AMP).
CHERUBINI:	*Requiem* (AMP, Sch.). A great work.
	Mass in C (Ka.).
MENDELSSOHN:	*St. Paul* (Sch., Ka.). Although not so well known as *Elijah,* this easier oratorio is a distinguished work.
	Hymn of Praise (Ka.).
VERDI:	*Stabat Mater* (Pe.). A beautiful work, written by the master during his last years (no solos).
BRAHMS:	*Nänie* (Sch., AMP). A short but profound work, not very difficult.
DVOŘÁK:	*Te Deum* (Ka.). A very fine work (two solos).

FRANCK:	*Solemn Mass* (Ka.).
	150th Psalm (AMP).
BRUCKNER:	*Te Deum* (Ka., Pe.). A great work, not easy.
FAURÉ:	*Requiem* (Sch.). One of the less difficult works of the period, but Fauré's style requires sensitivity.
	Pavane (Br.). May be played without chorus.
HOLST:	*Psalms* (Br.). Psalms 86 and 148.
HARRIS:	*Folksong* Symphony (Sch.).
HINDEMITH:	*Das Unaufhörliche* (AMP).
	In Praise of Music (AMP). A work written for amateurs; very effective.
	Let's Build a Town (AMP). Written for children, suitable for elementary schools.
VAUGHAN WILLIAMS:	*Serenade* (Oxford). Charming, not difficult.
DELLO JOIO:	*Three Songs of Chopin* (Marks). Definitely within the range of amateurs, and playable by orchestra alone.
MEYEROWITZ:	*Two Litanies* (Br.). With chamber orchestra.
HOVHANESS:	*Magnificat* (Pe.). An interesting work.

CHORUS AND BAND

There are many more bands in American colleges than orchestras, and the disproportion is even higher in the high schools. Works for chorus with wind instruments, listed below, should be especially welcome.

GABRIELI:	*Jubilate Deo* (Sch.). Eight-part chorus with brass.
GABRIELI-STOKOWSKI:	*In Excelsis* (Br.). Brass.
BACH:	Cantata No. 118 (Marks). The original was written for obsolete winds, for which in this edition contemporary instruments have been substituted.
MENDELSSOHN:	*Festival Hymn* (Br.). Male chorus and two brass choirs.
BRUCKNER:	Mass in E Minor (Br.). Brass. Difficult but worth performing.
HINDEMITH:	*Apparebit Repentina Dies* (AMP). Brass.
GRAINGER:	*I'm Seventeen Come Sunday* (Sch.). Brass.
	County Derry Air (Sch.). For women's or

men's chorus and band or orchestra. Not difficult.

MEYEROWITZ: *How Goodly is the House of God* (Br.). Brass.

LOCKWOOD: *The Closing Doxology* (Br.). High school and college level, with band.

One of the best ways to get chorus and instruments together (orchestra or band) is to use the vast quantity of choral music of the sixteenth and seventeenth centuries. Most of this music is generally known only as vocal music. It was, however, quite customary in those times to support the voices with strings or winds. Vocal or instrumental color hardly existed; clarity of the contrapuntal lines was paramount. As long as every voice is distinctly heard, and the structure sounds balanced, any combination may be used to sing and play the single voices. Instruments may even be substituted for middle and low parts in works containing more than four voices.

There is nothing extraordinary about this. Bach wrote his chorales for four voices supported by instruments – the soprano usually by first violins and higher woodwinds, the alto by second violins, the tenor by viola, and the bass by cello, bass, and bassoon. This distribution may serve as a guide. So long as they do not overpower the voices brasses may also be used.

Combining instruments with voices may be a good way to start an instrument group in schools. Whatever instruments are available may join the chorus, especially to supplement weaker vocal parts. It is also feasible to have a whole chorus (or part of it) played by instruments alone, as an introduction or an interlude. With taste and imagination excellent results may be achieved.

27

Band conducting

THERE is no great difference between the techniques of band and orchestra conducting, but a band director should have some training as an orchestra conductor. Important band music has been written by the best contemporary composers but the masterworks of instrumental music are orchestral. A limited number of pieces for band were written by masters in the classical and romantic periods, such as Handel's *Royal Fireworks Music*; the *Symphonie Funèbre et Triomphale* by Berlioz; the *Overture for Band* by Mendelssohn; and the Mass in E Minor for chorus and band by Bruckner. But none of these is equal in stature to the great symphonies of Mozart, Haydn, or Beethoven, and it is in the latter that the student can best learn the subtleties of conducting. The preponderance of percussion and brass, furthermore, though conducive to forceful and rhythmically precise execution, does not allow for the more refined sound qualities of an orchestral performance. True, band members have learned in recent years to play a pianissimo that can almost match a string pianissimo; but a conductor steeped in knowledge of the masterworks will achieve dynamic subtleties with greater ease.

Many of the standard classics have been transcribed for band, sometimes even in "digest" form. Purists reject this tampering with our musical heritage, and, unfortunately, many of these transcriptions do not reflect the beauty of the original. To demand that bands play only works written originally for bands, however, would prevent a large section of our younger generation from becoming familiar with the works of the masters. That is why band conductors should have enough knowledge of orchestral literature and of the original scores to know the difference between good and bad transcriptions.

Another reason why the band conductor ought to know orchestral styles is that the martellato and non-legato bowings of baroque music should be imitated by the wind instruments – as should the spiccato and even saltato of the later styles (see Part Three).

An orchestra conductor leading a band will have to get used to the different balance and volume of tone. In an orchestra each of the two clarinets plays different parts, but in a band they play in large groups, like the violin sections of an orchestra. There are a large number of brass and percussion instruments in a band, this requiring a different "ear." A good musician will adjust to this new sound. A band *can* play softly, and it *can* be trained to apply fine dynamic shadings. The time is past when the main purpose of a band was to play marches.

BAND SCORES

Full band scores are generally much larger than orchestra scores (see Chapter 10). The classical orchestra score seldom has more than twelve staves, the romantic score about sixteen, only very large modern scores have perhaps twenty-four; but that many or more are not unusual in a band score. For this reason band conductors prefer condensed scores. It should not be forgotten that the number of transposing instruments is much larger in a band. On the other hand, if the band conductor wants to have absolute control of his group he had better have a score in front of him (when it exists) that tells him exactly what each instrument is playing.

In an orchestra, strings usually predominate. In a band there are a number of independent groups, each large enough to form an entity of its own. Contemporary composers (who virtually originated the symphonic band) make use of this diversity to shift from group to group in main and secondary voices. This instrumental kaleidoscope must be clearly organized by the conductor. He must encourage the group that should prevail with a timely glance or motions of his left hand. Another detail requiring attention is the frequent change of dynamics. When a conductor attends to these matters the sound of his band will be clear and lucid.

SEATING

Seating a band, as seating an orchestra, depends upon the acoustics of the hall. In this respect there are two schools of thought. One considers the band a kind of transformed orchestra — flutes and clarinets for the violins, and bass clarinets, bassoons, or baritone saxophones for the cellos and basses. The high woodwinds are therefore seated to the left, the low to the right of the conductor.

The second school regards the band as an entity in its own right, with characteristics quite different from that of an orchestra. The seating is therefore changed, except that in both cases the heavy brass and percussion are seated in the rear. The high woodwinds are arranged in a semicircle around the conductor and the low ones are placed behind them. The horns, which because of the preponderance of heavy brass in a band are often too weak (in contrast to the orchestra), are placed wherever their tone cuts through best. When playing in a shell or with a rear wall that reflects the sounds, horns should be close to this resonant background. An orchestra conductor generally stands close to the strings but the band conductor stands at a more distant point, where he is better able to hear his more sonorous instruments.

MUSIC FOR BAND

A number of works for winds, written by the masters, was mentioned at the beginning of this chapter. Here are some additional works.

GABRIELI:	*Sonata Pian' e Forte.*
BEETHOVEN:	Military Marches.
MOZART:	Serenade (K. 361), for 13 wind instruments.
	Divertimentos (K. 167 and 168), for two flutes, five trumpets, and timpani.
GOSSEC:	*Ouverture in C.*
RICHARD STRAUSS:	Serenade, for 13 wind instruments.
	Two Military Marches.
DVOŘÁK:	Serenade, for winds, cellos, and basses.
RIMSKY-KORSAKOV:	Trombone and Band Concerto.

None of the works above belongs among the great masterpieces except the Mozart Serenade and the Gabrieli — and they are simply combinations of wind instruments, not band compositions.

The lack of great band music up to recent times accounts for the fact that a surprisingly large quantity of standard orchestral literature has been transcribed for band. Many of these transcriptions may be recommended because the spirit and even the texture of the original has been preserved. The great symphonies of the classical repertory, however, do not sound adequate when played without strings. Some have been arranged for band, but with very few exceptions they are better avoided. Many bands attempt, for instance, to play one of the most popular symphonies, Schubert's *Unfinished.* But much of its original tenderness is lost.

In the list that follows, transcriptions for band are suggested for the young conductor who wants to give his band a taste of the orchestral repertory. The grade of difficulty is indicated, but it should be realized that such grading cannot be entirely accurate. A piece may be difficult for one group of instruments and easy for another. Or it may be easy in general but have a difficult passage. The specifications — *e*: easy, *m*: medium, *d*: difficult — should serve, therefore, only as a broad guide. Publishers are indicated by the same abbreviations as in Chapter 26.

Marches, dances, etc.

BACH:	Chorales and piano works	*e-m*	Sch., Bo.
	Komm Suesser Tod	*e*	F.
BEETHOVEN:	*Turkish March* from *The Ruins of Athens*	*e-m*	F.
	Contredances	*e-m*	F.
BRAHMS:	*Hungarian Dances*	*m*	F., Bo.
	Choral preludes	*e-m*	AMP.
BERLIOZ:	*Hungarian March* from the *Damnation of Faust*	*e-m*	F., Bo.
	March to the Scaffold from *Symphonie Fantastique*	*m-d*	F.
BIZET:	*L'Arlésienne* suite	*m-d*	F., Bo.
BRITTEN:	*Soirées Musicales* (Rossini)	*m-d*	Bo.

Composer	Work	Grade	Publisher
CHABRIER:	España	*m-d*	F.
CHOPIN:	*Marche Joyeuse*	*m*	Bo.
	Military Polonaise	*e*	F., Bo.
DE FALLA:	Ritual Fire Dance from *El Amor Brujo*	*m-d*	Marks
ELGAR:	*Pomp and Circumstance* 1, 2, 4, 5	*m-d*	Bo.
GEMINIANI:	Andante	*e-m*	Colombo
IPPOLITOV-IVANOV:	*Caucasian Sketches*	*d*	F.
KABALEVSKY:	*Galop of the Comedians*	*m-d*	L.
KATCHATURIAN:	*Gayne* ballet	*m-d*	L.
	Galop from *Masquerade* suite	*d*	L.
LECOCQ-MOHAUPT:	*Madame Angot* ballet	*m-d*	AMP.
LISZT:	*Hungarian Rhapsody* No. 2	*d*	F., Bo.
MASCAGNI:	*Intermezzo* from *Cavalleria Rusticana*	*e*	F.
MASSENET:	*Aragonesa,* from *Le Cid* ballet	*e*	F.
	Scènes Napolitaines	*m-d*	F.
	Scènes Pittoresques	*m-d*	F., Bo.
MENDELSSOHN:	*War March of the Priests* from *Athalia*	*e.*	F.
MEYERBEER:	*Coronation March* from *The Prophet*	*m*	F., Bo.
	Torch Dance	*m*	F.
MOUSSORGSKY:	Coronation scene, from *Boris Godounov*	*m-d*	F.
	Pictures at an Exhibition	*d*	F.
	Gopak from *The Fair at Sorochinsk*	*m*	Bo.
PONCHIELLI:	*Dance of the Hours,* from *La Gioconda*	*m-d*	F.
PROKOFIEFF:	*Triumphal March,* from *Peter and the Wolf*	*m*	Marks
	March and scherzo, from *Love for Three Oranges*	*m-d*	Bo.
RACHMANINOV:	Preludes	*m*	F., Bo.
RESPIGHI:	*Pines of the Appian Way,* from *The Pines of Rome*	*m-d*	Colombo
RIMSKY-KORSAKOV:	*Song of India*	*e.*	F., Bo.
	Hymn to the Sun, from *Le Coq d'Or*	*e-m*	F., Bo.
	Capriccio Espagnol	*m-d*	F., Bo.

	The Young Prince and Princess from *Scheherazade*	*m-d*	F.
RUBINSTEIN:	*Kamenoi Ostrov*	*m*	F.
SAINT-SAENS:	*Bacchanale,* from *Samson and Delilah*	*d*	F.
	March Heroique	*m*	Bo.
SCHUBERT:	*Military Marches* 1, 2	*e-m*	Sch.
	Entr'acte and ballet music, from *Rosamunde*	*m*	Sch.
SIBELIUS:	*Finlandia*	*m-d*	F., Bo.
	Alla Marcia	*m*	Marks
J. STRAUSS:	Waltzes	*m-d*	F., Bo.
	Perpetuum Mobile	*d*	Bo.
TCHAIKOVSKY:	*Capriccio Italien*	*d*	F., Bo.
	Marche Slave	*d*	F.
	Nutcracker suite	*m-d*	F.
	Sleeping Beauty waltz	*m-d*	F., Bo.
	Petite Suite	*m-d*	Marks
VERDI:	*Grand March,* from *Aida*	*e-m*	F.
	Anvil Chorus, from *Il Trovatore*	*e*	F.
VIVALDI:	Concerto for Two Trumpets and Band	*e-m*	Colombo
	Concerto for Piccolo and Band	*e-m*	Colombo
WAGNER:	*Sailors' Chorus,* from *The Flying Dutchman*	*e-m*	F.
	Elsa Entering the Cathedral, from *Lohengrin*	*e*	F.
	Entry of the Gods to Vallhall from *Das Rheingold*	*m*	F., Bo.
	Pilgrims' Chorus, from *Tannhäuser*	*e*	F.
	Wotan's Farewell, and *Magic Fire Music,* from *Die Walküre*	*m-d*	F.
WEBER:	Invitation to the Dance	*m-d*	F.

Overtures

ADAM:	*If I were King*	*e-m*	F.

BEETHOVEN:	*Coriolanus*	*m-d*	F., Bo.
	Egmont	*m-d*	F., Bo.
BRAHMS:	*Academic Festival*	*d*	F.
FLOTOW:	*Martha*	*m*	F., Bo.
	Alessandro Stradella	*m*	F.
GLINKA:	*A Life for the Tsar*	*d*	F.
HÉROLD:	*Zampa*	*m-d*	Bo.
OFFENBACH:	*La Belle Hélène*	*m-d*	Sch.
ROSSINI:	Overtures	*m-d*	F., Bo.
SCHUBERT:	*Rosamunde*	*m-d*	Bo.
SCHUMANN:	*Festival*	*e-m*	F.
SMETANA:	*Libuša*	*m*	F.
SUPPÉ:	*Light Cavalry*	*m-d*	F., Bo.
	Beautiful Galatea	*m*	F.
	Pique Dame	*m*	F., Bo.
	Poet and Peasant	*m-d*	F., Bo.
SULLIVAN:	*Iolanthe*	*m*	F.
	The Pirates of Penzance	*m*	F.
THOMAS:	*Mignon*	*m-d*	F.
	Raymond	*m-d*	F., Bo.
TCHAIKOVSKY:	*1812*	*d*	Bo.
VERDI:	*La Forza del Destino*	*m-d*	F.
	Nabucco	*m*	F.
WAGNER:	*Lohengrin,* Act Three	*d*	F., Bo.
	Rienzi	*d*	F., Bo.
	Die Meistersinger	*d*	Bo.

Symphonic works

BORODIN:	Symphony No. 2 in B Minor, first movement	*d*	F.
DVORAK:	Symphony, *From the New World,* Largo and Finale	*m-d*	F.

Interest in band music has sharply risen during the last fifty years, and composers have been more inclined to write for this medium. Composers of serious music presently write almost as many works for band as for orchestra. New works appear on the market almost every day; works that are meant to be played by school and college bands, in contrast to orchestral works, which are generally written for professional groups. Below are some of the important works of this century – works that paved the way for acceptance of the band as a serious musical organization.

Paul Hindemith, while still in Germany, wrote *Concert Music for Wind Orchestra,* as well as *Concert Music for Piano, Brass, and Harp*; in this country he composed *Symphony for Band* (AMP), his most important work of this kind (but also a rather complicated one).

Darius Milhaud wrote *Suite Française* (L.), a delightful work within the range of any competent concert band. Stravinsky, in his *Symphony for Band,* employs a number of instruments generally not found in a band (bass flute, English horn.) Prokofieff composed marches for band, Villa Lobos, *Concerto Grosso for Wind Quartet and Wind Orchestra.* Poulenc composed *Aubade* for piano and eighteen wind instruments, and Křenek, *Symphony for Wind and Percussion,* three *Jolly Marches,* and *Kleine Blasmusik.* There are also a number of works by Gustav Holst (Bo.) and Vaughan Williams.

American composers more than any others have, in the last twenty years, turned out band music in increasing quantity (see *Workbook*). They, too, have been investigating and studying the inner workings of the band, and many have contributed to making band music an integral part of musical literature. Due at least in part to these efforts the American concert band has recently made enormous progress.

28 *Accompanying a soloist*

WHEN a soloist performs with the orchestra, the conductor is no longer the center of attraction. It is as an accompanist, however, that he can show his technique and musicianship, and his ability to conduct with an "open ear." Flexibility, feeling for style, knowledge of the technique of the solo instrument (or of the vocal problems of a singer), all are required for conducting an accompaniment.

The conductor should know every note of the solo part. If, for instance, the soloist has a long passage that runs into an orchestral entrance, the conductor must be able to anticipate the exact moment when the orchestra comes in.

THE SOLOIST

If the soloist is a professional, it is the duty of the conductor to *accompany* him, that is to subordinate tempo, phrasing, and dynamics to the wishes of the soloist. There may be places where he does not agree with the soloist's conception; he should discuss the matter with him – but not in front of the orchestra. Some singers, for example, have the bad habit of holding fermatas, on any high note, to show off their voice. The conductor should tactfully try to remedy such procedures, which often are in bad taste. Nevertheless, he usually will accept the soloist's interpretation as it is.

Matters are different when the performer is a student. Then the conductor should – in rehearsals with the student and if possible with the student's teacher present – get the tempo set, as well as other matters of interpretation. He may even lead the student, who in his excitement and inexperience may not adhere to the conception of the work agreed upon. On the other hand, if because of nervousness the soloist sets his own tempo *during a performance* the conductor must follow him diligently even if he disapproves. The necessity of "improvising" a tempo at the last moment, of subordinating oneself to a soloist, affords excellent training for any young conductor – or orchestra. Here both can show their flexibility.

Even professional soloists sometimes have the nervous habit of speeding up when they have fast runs. A sensitive conductor will soon notice this and anticipate this speeding up and thus always be able to fit his accompaniment to the soloist. In the interest of a "clean" performance — though this habit shows a lack of solid musicianship — the conductor must subject himself to such whims of the soloist.

At certain times the soloist must watch the beat of the conductor. This happens when both soloist and orchestra have the first attack or when they start together after a fermata. Good examples are: the second and last movements of Bach's Concerto for Two Violins; the last movements of Brahms's Violin Concerto, Second Piano Concerto, and Double Concerto and the second movement of Beethoven's First Piano Concerto. When the soloist alone has an upbeat (between beats) before the entrance of the orchestra, he should watch carefully for the conductor's preparatory beat before the orchestral attack. Example: Mozart: B-flat Major Piano Concerto, K. 450, finale. Other examples are the last movements of Mozart's Horn Concertos, K. 495 and K. 447; and Beethoven's Violin Concerto, last movement (here the orchestra starts right after first beat); the third movement of Prokofieff's Second Violin Concerto. Some examples of a start after a fermata are Liszt's First Piano Concerto and Prokofieff's Third Piano Concerto (third variation).

In the Liszt concerto there is another dangerous spot. In the last section there is a fermata, after which a martial 4/4 tempo starts. The first half measure of this new tempo consists of a rest (two beats); then the solo piano rushes in with sixteenths, while the full orchestra enters on the fourth beat. The two first beats (on the rest) should be given very sharply by the conductor, and the soloist must watch him carefully in order to come in exactly on time.

When the soloist has a cadenza that ends on a trill, the finishing turn of which leads to the entrance of the orchestra, the soloist must also wait for the conductor's upbeat before playing the afterbeat.

CADENZAS

The conductor should apply a special kind of beat for cadenzas and solo interludes. When the orchestra has a single fermata for the whole cadenza the conductor should let his baton rest until the end, then give the necessary starting beat. During solos, however, orchestra parts often have a number of rest measures. There are two ways to handle this problem: Either the conductor beats — very unobtrusively — every downbeat, or he tells the orchestra when he will start beating again. The latter method is preferable when the solo is long and the orchestra enters at a clearly discernable place, especially if the tempo changes at that spot. (Examples: Liszt's piano concertos.)

Another tricky attack occurs in the finale of Beethoven's Violin Concerto after the cadenza. The orchestra has a fermata on a rest during the cadenza. This cadenza ends with a trill on E, upon which the metered measures start again in the orchestra — but no instrument begins to play before the end of the second measure. The conductor must start beating exactly on the first trill measure, even though nothing happens in the orchestra, because the players will have to count from that measure on. Other instruments enter later. If they have had no chance to count their measures they may easily get lost.

When the orchestra plays only on the first beats the conductor should not give every beat in each measure. He would appear to be conducting the soloist. It is better to give only the downbeats. The same procedure is used when the orchestra holds notes through two or more measures, which happens frequently in classical concertos. All the conductor has to do is give very subtle downbeats on each new measure. When the orchestra plays more notes in each measure he returns to the usual beat-pattern. Even then, during the soloist's passages, subtlety is called for. Composers generally orchestrate accompaniments so the orchestra will not cover important sections of the solo. Should the orchestration occasionally be too heavy, slight dynamic retouches may be called for. The conductor should be aware, however, that sometimes the orchestra has the more important part and the soloist the accompaniment. The soloist should always be clearly audible, but one should remember that concertos are written not for solo with orchestral accompaniment but for solo *and* orchestra. The soloist is the center of attraction but the orchestra is meant to be more than a mere shadow.

29

Conducting opera and operetta

THIS country has a limited operatic tradition. Aside from the Metropolitan Opera there have been very few opera companies. The general public has been slow to appreciate opera, partly because it is almost always sung in a foreign language. True, some of the original style is lost in translation, but countries with great operatic traditions, like Italy, Germany, and France all perform operas in their own languages. Verdi is sung in German in Germany and French in France, *Carmen* is sung in Italian in Italy. The argument that English is not a suitable language for opera is based on prejudice. Mozart's *Marriage of Figaro,* originally composed in Italian, can be done as well in a good English translation as in a German one.

What makes the fact that there are so few first-class opera companies in this country especially deplorable is the unusual amount of good opera-singing talent in America – material that goes to waste. Young singers frequently must go to Europe to gain experience. But many cannot afford to leave; those who remain are exploited by clever impresarios who produce operas all over America with second-class equipment, inadequate orchestras (if any), and slipshod preparation. Young singers sometimes even pay in return for the "experience." Schools and colleges, on the other hand, have created opera workshops, and, when headed by capable conductors and stage directors, have done remarkable work. Opera in English is gradually being accepted (even at the Metropolitan), as the best way to make opera popular. In some American universities and colleges these opera workshops have achieved amazingly high standards, with performances that may be favorably compared to Europe.

The growing acceptance of opera in America has also resulted in the formation of an increasing number of small professional companies. Many have achieved a high level of accomplishment, helped by foundations and opera lovers. Like the opera workshops in colleges, however, their output is limited to two, three, at best four operas a year, each one performed only once or a few times, whereas a European municipal company has a repertory of twenty or thirty. This is deplorable because a competent production requires immense efforts: months of hard work in coaching singers, rehearsing the orchestra, staging, costuming, constructing the scenery and then rehearsing the combined forces, to mention only a few details. Nevertheless, a good start has been made; opera is now definitely on its way in the United States.

But the rapid growth of interest in opera has also had its drawbacks. High schools have begun to perform *Carmen, Cavalleria Rusticana, The Marriage of Figaro, Rigoletto,* and even *Madama Butterfly* and *Faust.* Ambitious young conductors should avoid them. They require mature voices, well trained and secure. It is true that some young singers show remarkable talent at an early age; but casting them in roles such as Santuzza, Butterfly, or Carmen will do them more harm than good. The operas mentioned are so full of well-known tunes that audiences are thrilled to hear them performed by youngsters, but this enthusiasm should not influence a young conductor's better judgment. There are so many operas suitable for high school and college performances, written within the range of young singers, that there is no need to attempt the great repertory works. There are still the Gilbert and Sullivan standbys — let there be no snobbery about them. They are fine works, and they can be done very well or very badly. They lend themselves excellently to good staging and singing.

PRODUCING AN OPERA

In recent years the number of operas suitable for school use has grown immensely, partly thanks to new works written by American composers, partly because of usable translations of European works. Some guiding principles may be valuable.*

Choose an opera only after the abilities of all prospective soloists are known. Type-cast in cooperation with the stage di-

* The Central Opera Service, connected to the Metropolitan Opera Company, has a list of all works available. It also furnishes information on castings, length, and necessary stage sets. The conductor who wants to keep abreast with what is going on in the field should register with this service.

rector. If the opera is a difficult one, arrange for ample rehearsal time.

An opera loses a great deal, of course, if it is not presented with orchestra, but if the players cannot cope with it there is no choice; the performance should not be spoiled by an inadequate instrumental group. Sometimes two pianos are a fair substitute (but clearly a substitute). The conductor may have to make his own arrangement for two pianos from the full score. Piano and a few instruments are even better. It is vital that the conductor master orchestration if he is to make the necessary arrangement. (Some operas are available with reduced orchestrations.)

Very often orchestra material for operas, especially operettas, will be found to be in bad condition – badly written, full of mistakes, with different parts having different cuts. These matters should all be corrected before the first orchestra rehearsal. Add rehearsal numbers or letters to the parts if there are not enough.

If the opera has a chorus there must be sufficient time for choral rehearsal. At least three hours a week for the chorus alone will be necessary. If soloists are to sing with the chorus, they should join in as soon as the chorus is secure. Continue these ensemble rehearsals until the cast is completely familiar with the music – bearing in mind that on stage they will be distracted by the action. Sometimes they may not even see the conductor's beat. (Nothing labels a performance as amateurish quite so fast as when singers on stage have their eyes constantly glued to the baton.) Meanwhile, solo parts should be rehearsed thoroughly with piano; if the conductor is a good enough pianist he might coach them himself, at least in the beginning. The chorus should have an accompanist from the start.

As soon as the orchestra knows its parts fairly well a joint rehearsal should be held, in which the soloists merely listen in order to become familiar with the orchestral sound. The orchestra may have passages that the singers have not heard in the piano score. The next step is to combine orchestra and voices, without acting. The chorus too should have at least one non-acting rehearsal with the orchestra. In order to get used to the actual sound, it should *stand* on stage.

To conduct an opera the conductor must be *entirely* familiar with the score. He should know it from memory, including the words of the singers. This is not a difficult task; with so many rehearsals he can hardly fail to remember every note. During the actual performance the conductor's main attention must be directed to the stage. The orchestra has its music in front of it, but the singers sing from memory. With the added excitement and distractions, they will need all the help the conductor can give. It should be made clear to the players if they are accustomed to receiving cues, that they must not depend on it; the primary concern has to be for the singers.

MISHAPS

In a well-trained orchestra rarely anything goes wrong during a performance, however, there is seldom an opera performance in which the conductor is not called upon to deal with an emergency of some kind. It is here that an opera conductor can show his skill — and here that he will reap the benefit if he has trained his group to follow the beat constantly (see Chapters 2 and 4). A singer may have missed a cue and come in late; then the conductor must wait with his down beat until the singer has caught up. If the orchestra knows that it must *always* follow the conductor — especially that it must not play the first beat of any measure before it gets the downbeat — disaster can be averted. If the singer is ahead, the conductor will have to quicken his beat to catch up. It may happen that the singer is off entirely. Then the conductor must do all the adjusting; he must have the presence of mind to survey the situation quickly and decide where stage and orchestra should be brought together again. Occasionally, a drastic procedure may be required: the conductor may have to stop the orchestra and call out (as softly as possible) a nearby rehearsal number. The orchestra will then come in on that measure.

A skilled leader can do all this very quietly, and have such unpleasant episodes go practically unnoticed. In general, incidents like this will not happen in well-prepared performances. They should be the *rare* exception to the rule. But the conductor must be *ready* for them. A major disaster may occur if he gets flustered.

THE BEAT

Opera conducting is in many ways similar to accompanying a soloist in a concert. When the orchestra does not actually play, when the singer has a few measures of unaccompanied recitative, give a clear downbeat for each measure. Often, during a recitative, the orchestra will have a single chord. If it occurs on a downbeat there is no problem; but frequently it is on an offbeat – the second, the fourth, or between beats. Some conductors give these chords – wherever they occur – on downbeats. This is a bad habit and confusing to those who have rests. They lose count. In a recitative the beginning of a measure should be given on a downbeat, even when there is a rest. There is no reason why, because the chord happens to be on a second beat, the conductor cannot follow the normal beat-pattern and give this beat (in 4/4 meter) with a clear motion from the middle to the left (prepared by the first beat).

In some operas music accompanies spoken words. Occasionally, the composer will indicate the exact rhythm (Puccini: *Gianni Schicchi, La Rondine*). When it is not indicated it is up to the conductor to listen carefully and see to it that the music fits the spoken words it accompanies (Massenet: *Manon;* Beethoven: *Fidelio;* Weber: *Der Freischütz;* Weill: *Down in the Valley;* Wilder: *The Lowland Sea*).

During the performance the conductor will frequently need his left hand, not only for giving cues to the singers but for quieting the orchestra. The acoustic conditions in the auditorium must be extremely favorable if the orchestra, playing the printed dynamic signs, is not to drown out the voices. The orchestra can prove its ability here by achieving a good piano; the brass (even when a forte is indicated) should refrain from blaring; accentuation with a kind of *fp* or at least *fmf* will give the impression of an energetic and lively orchestra. (To have it play softly throughout would make the orchestra sound anemic.) In forte passages where *no* singing is going on, whether for a number of measures or only a few notes, the orchestra may play full force, and in this way add to the impact of the drama. These places should be marked in the parts and the players made aware of them at rehearsals; still, the conductor will often need his left hand to keep the orchestra dynamically in check.

ELECTRONIC AIDS

To facilitate staging, the following device has proved a great help: record all the music (with piano accompaniment) on tape as soon as the singers are familiar with their parts. The stage director may then block the action with the singers while the recording is being played. This will save the singers' voices, which are apt to be strained during stage rehearsals, and allow them to keep their minds entirely on the action. The constant repetition of the music while they adjust their movements will implant it in their memories, and most important, the staging can begin even before the singers have memorized their parts. Meanwhile the purely musical rehearsals should be continued in order to improve the singing — which most likely will gain in purpose when the singers know their actions. Eventually, when they know their parts by heart, they can "mouth" them while the tape recorder plays. Finally, when their actions are all set and they no longer have to concentrate on every step, they should be able to sing without straining.

Another use for an electronic device is to have the orchestral sound "piped" on stage. Singers — especially in an ensemble —

are frequently unable to hear the orchestra well enough for sufficient support. Ordinarily they depend chiefly on the beat of the conductor, and are thus forced to keep looking at him.*

Do not amplify voices if it can be avoided. Public address systems should only be used in emergencies.

Most important, the conductor must be clearly visible to the cast as well as the orchestra. Good lighting is necessary. The musicians' lighting fixtures should throw light on the music only – they should not distract the audience.†

THE ORCHESTRA

Young musicians at an operatic performance may feel somewhat frustrated if they cannot see what is happening on stage. They should be invited to attend one of the last rehearsals with piano. During dress rehearsals and performances, however, their attention must be focused exclusively on the music in front of them. It would be inexcusable if – after a dialogue on stage or a rest in a particular part – someone missed his attack. In opera the orchestra is relegated to a lesser role than in concert. Cooperation is needed for the success of the enterprise. A colorful and effective opera production can and should be such a stirring experience that anyone taking part in it has reason for pride.

No young conductor should start an opera workshop without previous experience or experienced help. He needs a stage director qualified to stage opera, which is a skill in itself. Timing, range, and purpose of the action have to be coordinated with the pace and character of the music. An opera stage director needs thorough musical as well as dramatic training.

* The stage director should plan all action so that singers face the conductor when they *must* see the beat. Young singers must learn to watch the leader with the corner of the eye, even when addressing someone on stage. Training is needed to achieve this, however.

† The sides and top of the conductor's stand should be bent to hide fluorescent light bulbs on three sides. The outside should be black, the inside painted with white enamel for reflection. This way the inside is well lit without any light being seen from the audience.

Music Suitable for Non-professional Orchestras

Appendix

THE material to follow is a survey of orchestral music suitable for performance by school, college, and amateur groups. Such a compilation could easily fill a large volume. Condensation has been necessary but the survey should nevertheless be helpful to the conductor entering the field.

A large number of "folios" for orchestra, intended for elementary and higher grades, has been published. These vary in their musical value and their fitness for beginners. Most have only a condensed (piano) score, often without cues concerning orchestration. There are newer editions, fortunately, which furnish full scores. There is a growing realization that even elementary music teachers should have the background to be able to use them. Conductors will be much more efficient when they can check every note each instrument should play.

Many folios are compiled with the commendable idea of familiarizing young students with "gems" of great music as early as possible. This worthy purpose is impaired, however, when pieces are included that can be played only at half the original tempo. The young teacher with good musical taste will avoid pieces that tamper with great music, at least to the extent that playing them would do more damage than good to the musical education of his group. To be sure, compromises have to be made – compromises at which a purist will frown. Original keys may be changed, or instruments used (saxophones, trombones, percussion) that the composer never dreamed of. The "gems" may be arranged in "medleys" with crude transitions. The recommendations to follow are "middle-of-the-road." A rigid approach would have eliminated most of the folios. Those selected do serve the purpose, although sometimes very good pieces and questionable ones are to be found in the same folio. Those considered altogether below standard are not included.

Folios should be supplemented with single pieces to fit the level of the group. The wide area of baroque music is highly appropriate for a solid orchestral foundation, although it belongs to a period somewhat removed from a modern youngster's feeling and imagination. It is extremely "educational," but music of later times should be added – if possible – even contemporary music.

Numbers 1-7 are used to define the grade of the music: 1 is easy, 4 medium, 7 difficult. The survey does not go beyond the scope of a good college or amateur orchestra and pieces suitable only for professional orchestras are *not* included.

In folios or works with more than one movement, some pieces are often much easier than others. In such cases a classification such as 2-4 or 3-7 is used, showing that some belong to a lower and some to a higher category. In one-movement pieces, some instruments may have more difficult passages than others; here, too, the wider designation is employed.

At times an augmentation of the original orchestration is possible, and for schools it is often advisable. Such pieces are marked "exp." for expandable. Needless to say these additions have to be made in good musical taste.

Music for School and Amateur Orchestras

Title	*Publisher*	*Grade*	*Score*
First Orchestra Album	Mills	1	Piano
The More the Merrier	Bourne	1	Piano
Orff: *Schulwerk* (*Music for Children*) (4 vols.)	AMP (Schott)	1	Full
Mostly percussion instruments with singing.*			

* A thoroughly methodical approach to teaching melody, harmony, and rhythm in elementary schools.

Music Educators' Elementary Orchestra Album	Mills	1-2	Full
Beginners' Orchestra Folio	Rubank	1-2	Piano
Exercises and pieces.			
Easy Steps to the Orchestra	Mills	1-2	Full
Classroom Concert	Belwin	1-2	Piano
Mostly folksongs.			
Palmer-Best: *The First Year in the Orchestra*	Oxford	1-2	Piano
Strings.			
The Belwin Orchestra Builder	Oxford	1-2	Piano
Isaacs-Weber: *Orchestra Rehearsal Fundamentals*	Oxford	1-3	Piano
Good help for the teacher.			
Music for Young Orchestras	Fischer	1-3	Full
Playing in the Orchestra	Bourne	1-3	Piano
Folklore and "gems."			
Our Own Orchestra Folio	Fischer	1-3	Piano
Merle Isaacs' Orchestra Folio	Belwin	1-3	Piano
Good classics and Isaacs' originals.			
Over the Bridge	Belwin	1-3	Piano
Good beginners' folklore.			
Americana Collection	Rubank	1-3	Piano
Little Classic Orchestra Folio	Presser	1-3	Piano
Mostly classical piano pieces, well orchestrated.			
Woodhouse Folio	Boosey	1-3	Piano
National Songs for Assembly	Fischer	1-3	Piano
Living Music from the Past	Fischer	1-3	Full
Baroque music and one Mozart piece (full orchestrations).			
We Want Music	Ricordi	2-4	Piano
Great Themes for Orchestra	Bourne	2-5	Full
Concert Folio	Bourne	2-5	Full
From baroque to contemporary.			
Orchestra Program Album (3 vols.)	Mills	2-5	Full
Modern Masters Orchestra Album	Rubank	2-5	Cond. score
Good selection except Wagner's *Huldigungs Marsch,* his weakest work.			

Music for School and Amateur Orchestras (*cont'd.*)

Title	*Publisher*	*Grade*	*Score*
*Master Series for Young Orchestras:**			
Classic Dance Suite	Schirmer	2-5	Full
Masterworks for String Orchestra	Leeds	2-5	Full
Good baroque music.			
Educational Orchestra Album (3 vols.)	Fischer	2-5	Piano
Includes Ravel's *Pavane.*			
Living Music from the Past	Fischer	2-5	Full
Contains early Mozart symphony.			
String Music of the Baroque Era	Boston	2-5	Full
Exp.			
Orchestra Folio (Isaacs)	Belwin	2-6	Full
Presser's Youth Orchestra Folio	Pressner	2-6	Piano
Will acquaint young orchestras with great music in "digest" form.			
Advancement Orchestra Folio	Fischer	2-6	Piano
Orchestra Transcriptions (1 & 2)	Mills	2-6	Cond. score
Good cross-cuings; many complete works, especially in Part 2.			
Progressive Orchestra Folio (4 vols.)	Fischer	2-7	Piano
Fine selection; but Mozart's *Cosí Fan Tutte* overture is difficult even for professionals.			
Fox Old Masters Folio	Fox	2-6	Piano
Classics for Orchestra	Bourne	3-5	Piano
Distinguished Music (Taylor)	Schirmer	3-6	Cond. score
Good selection.			
Album of Famous Waltzes	Ascher	3-6	Piano
Good selection, simplified orchestration.			
Music of Our Time	Fischer	3-6	Piano
Contemporary Americans, not "atonal."			
Rogers & Hammerstein Orchestra Folio	Williamson	3-6	Piano
Some very popular pieces.			
Golden Key Orchestra Series	Presser	3-6	Piano
Bach to late romantics.			

* This series also has albums devoted to Bach, Handel, Haydn, Mozart, Beethoven, Schubert, Weber, Mendelssohn, Schumann, Grieg, and Tchaikovsky, all very useful. Especially recommended: Haydn, Schumann. None is as easy as the *Classic Dance Suite.*

Great Moments in Music	Leeds	3-7	Full
Corelli to Milhaud.			
Pucciniana Fantasy	Ricordi	4-6	Full
Medleys from Puccini operas, simplified orchestration.			
We Want Music	Mills	4-6	Piano
Popular masterworks, some in "digest"' form.			

Single Pieces

Haydn: *Twelve Deutsche Tänze*	Bärenreiter	1-4	Full
Very charming and simple.			
Haydn: *Zehn Menuette* (Ten Minuets)	Bärenreiter	1-4	Full
Very simple.			
Lully: *Gavotte*	Presser	2-3	Full
Ditson Concert series (a good series)			
Gluck: *Gavotte*	Presser	2-3	Full
Ditson Concert Series.			
Handel: *Largo*	Presser	2-3	Full
Ditson Concert Series.			
Michael Haydn: *Pastorello*	Peters	2-3	Full
Bach-Clarke: *Bach for Strings*	Schirmer	2-4	Full
Ten short pieces for strings.			
Bach: Twelve Chorales	Schirmer	2-4	Piano
Haydn: *Chorale* and *Minuet*	Marks	2-4	Piano
Gluck: *Hymn to Diana,* from *Iphigenia in Tauris*	Fox	3	Full
Full modern orchestration of this classical work.			
Mendelssohn: *Venetian Boat Song*	Marks	3	Full
Bach: *Bourrée* and *Gavotte*	Presser	2-4	Full
Ditson Concert Series.			
Martini: *Gavotte Célèbre*	Presser	2-4	Full
Ditson Concert Series.			
Brahms: *Two Waltzes*	Presser	2-4	Full
Ditson Concert Series.			
Bizet: *Intermezzo* from *L'Arlésienne*	Presser	2-4	Full
Ditson Concert Series.			
Rimsky-Korsakov: *Song of India*	Presser	2-4	Full
Ditson Concert Series.			
Three Morris Dances	Presser	2-4	Full
Ditson Concert Series.			
Humperdinck: *Selections from Hänsel and Gretel*	Fischer	2-4	Piano
Well-known folk tunes from the popular opera.			

Music for School and Amateur Orchestras (*cont'd.*)

Title	*Publisher*	*Grade*	*Score*
Gluck: *Overture* to *Don Juan* (ballet)	Schirmer	2-4	Full
Simplified (first grade) second violin and bass parts. Arranged by this author.			
Brahms: *Three Songs*	Boosey	2-4	Full
Haydn: *Toy Symphony*	Boosey	2-4	Piano
Always an amusing piece.			
Martin: *Come to the Fair*	Boosey	2-4	Piano
Popular.			
Blow: *Overture and Ground in D minor*	Oxford	2-4	Full
Early baroque.			
Hertel: *Largo* and *Presto* from *Symphony in G*	Oxford	2-4	Full
Simple eighteenth century.			
Mendelssohn: *Dance of the Clowns* from *A Midsummer Night's Dream*	Oxford	3	Full
A "folksy" piece			
Gluck: *Three Festival Marches*	Peters	2-4	Full
Six horns, but substitution possible.			
Schumann: *Träumerei*	Witmark	3	Piano
Handel-Anderson: *Song* from *Semele*	Mills	3	Full
Moussorgsky: *Love Music* from *Boris Godounov*	Mills	3	Piano
A short piece.			
Gould: *Crinoline and Lace*	Mills	3	Piano
Gould: *Tropical*	Mills	3	Piano
The British Grenadiers	Mills	3	Piano
Well-known tune; fun.			
Arne: *Jig*	Mills	3	Full
Very useful.			
Alfen: *Swedish Polka*	Mills	2-4	Piano
Grainger: *County Derry Air*	Schirmer	2-5	Full
"Elastic" orchestration.			
Gluck: *At the Court of Maria Theresa*	Schirmer	2-5	Full
Simplified second violin and bass (Kahn).			
Dittersdorf: *Tournament of Temperaments*	Schirmer	2-5	Full
Simplified second violin and bass (Kahn).			
Handel: *Water Music Suite*	Schirmer	2-5	Full
Simplified second violin and bass (Kahn).			

Work	Publisher	Grade	Score
Beethoven: *Twelve Contredances* Original.	AMP	2-5	Full
Schubert: *Moment Musical* Ditson Concert Series.	Presser	2-5	Full
Schubert: *Ballet Music* (No. 2), from *Rosamunde* Ditson Concert Series.	Presser	2-5	Full
Bartok: *Five Pieces for Young Orchestra* Very "elastic" orchestration.	Remick	3-4	Full
Cowell: *Persian Set* Contemporary American (rental).	Peters	2-5	Full
Rosenmüller: *Sonatas* Strings; bowings and dynamics to be added (exp.).	Peters	2-5	Full
Field: *Rondo* Strings (exp.).	Oxford	3-4	Full
Bach: *Sheep May Safely Graze* Two flutes, strings, piano; very fine work.	Oxford, Fischer	3-4	Full
Bach: *Sinfonia* from Cantata *Wir danken dir, Gott* Strings, three trumpets (not too high), piano (organ) difficult.	Oxford	3-4	Full
Haydn: *Divertimento*	Bärenreiter	3-4	Full
Haydn: *Notturno No. 1, in C*	Bärenreiter	3-4	Full
Couperin-Milhaud: *Overture* and *Allegro*, from *La Sultana* Large orchestra.	Elkan-Vogel	2-5	Full
Foster: *Suite of Morris Dance Tunes* Light music.	Oxford	3-4	Full
Purcell: *Two Suites* from *The Fairy Queen* Strings; bowings needed (exp.).	Peters	2-5	Full
Mozart: *Five Contredances* Flute, snare drum, strings (exp.).	Peters	2-5	Full
Starer: *Dalton Set for Young People* Moderate contemporary.	Leeds	2-5	Full
Schubert: *Fünf Deutsche mit Coda* Strings (exp.).	AMP	2-5	Full
Schubert: *Waltzes* Arranged	Boosey		Full
Beethoven: *Sechs Ländlerische Tänze* Strings (exp.).	AMP	2-5	Full
Gould: *Pavane* A modern "classic."	Mills	2-5	Piano

Music for School and Amateur Orchestras (*cont'd.*)

Title	*Publisher*	*Grade*	*Score*
Lecuona: *Cordoba*	Marks	3-4	Piano
Riegger: *Suite for Younger Orchestras*	AMP	2-5	Cond. score
Interesting new approach by a contemporary American.			
Frescobaldi: *Toccata*	Mills	2-5	Piano
Baroque music in modern orchestration.			
Torroba: *Gardens of Granada*	Marks	3-4	Piano
Smetana: *Slavonic Lullaby,* from *The Kiss*	Boosey	3-4	Piano
Very sensitive, beautiful piece.			
Handel: *Rodelinda Overture* and *Terpsichore Suite*	Peters	2-6	Full
Two oboes, strings, harpsichord or piano (exp.).			
Humperdinck: *Dream Pantomime* and *Evening Prayer* from *Hansel and Gretel*	Fischer	3-5	Full
Farina: *Pavana e Gagliarda*	Peters	2-6	Full
Baroque. Strings (exp.).			
A. Scarlatti: *Concerto in F*	Peters	2-6	Full
Very fine piece (strings).			
Pepusch: Overture to *The Beggar's Opera*	Oxford	4	Full
Arranged.			
Cowell: *Ballad for String Orchestra*	AMP	4	Full
Contemporary American.			
Moussorgsky: *The Great Gate of Kiev*	Fitzsimons	3-5	Full
Large orchestra; contains caesuras.			
Handel-Beecham: *Amaryllis*	Boosey	3-5	Full
Full orchestra, no trombones.			
Handel: *Suite of Airs and Dances*	Peters	3-5	Full
Strings and piano (exp.).			
Bach-Stokowski: *Komm, Süsser Tod*	Broude	4	Full
Large orchestra; one of Bach's finest songs.			
Bach-Stokowski: *Chorale* from *Easter Cantata*	Broude	4	Full
Tchaikovsky: *Chanson Triste* and *Humoresque*	Boosey	4	Piano
Arrangement of these well-known pieces.			
J. C. Bach: Overture to *Lucio Silla*	Peters	3-5	Full
Classic orchestration; first violins somewhat difficult.			
Handel: *Suite* from *Julius Caesar*	Marks	3-5	Piano

Wagner: *Prize Song* from *Die Meistersinger*	Fischer	3-5	Full
Verdi: *Grand March* from *Aida*	Fox	3-5	Piano
Grainger: *Danish Folk Music Settings*	Schirmer	3-5	Piano
"Elastic" orchestration.			
Grainger: *Country Gardens*	Schirmer	3-5	Piano
"Elastic" orchestration.			
Grainger: *Spoon River*	Schirmer	4	Piano
"Elastic" orchestration.			
Guion: *Alley Tunes*	Schirmer	3-5	Piano
American tunes.			
Guion: *Sheep and Goat*	Schirmer	3-5	Piano
Effective.			
Sibelius: *Valse triste*	Schirmer	3-5	Piano
Strauss: *Annen Polka*	Boosey	4	Piano
L. Anderson: Pieces, e.g., *Syncopated Clock, Fiddle Faddle*	Mills	2-7	mostly piano
Various ranges of difficulty; ask publisher for particulars.			
Gould: *American Salute*	Mills	4-5	Piano
Effective.			
Gould: *Hillbilly*	Fischer	4-5	Piano
Delius: *Prelude* to *Irmelin*	Boosey	4-5	Full
Soft and tender.			
Cowell: *Hymn and Fuguing Tune*	AMP	4-5	Full
Strings.			
Thomas: *Zweite Spielmusik*	AMP	3-6	Full
"Elastic" orchestration; sprightly, neo-classic dances.			
S. W. Müller: *Weihnachtsmusik*	AMP	3-6	Full
Woodwinds, strings, Hindemith style, but simpler.			
Atterberg: *Suite Pastorale in Modo Antico*	AMP	3-6	Full
Strings; like Grieg's *Holberg Suite,* but easier.			
Cazden: *Six Definitions*	AMP	3-6	Full
In No. 2, meter changes make good conducting exercise.			
Hindemith: *Tafelmusik* (*Plöner Musiktag*)	AMP	3-6	Full
Written for students; intonation not easy.			
Hindemith: *Abendkonzert*	AMP	3-6	Full
In three parts. Arrangement is left to conductor.			
Clementi: *Symphony in B-flat Major*	Ricordi	4-5	Full
Like Mozart, but requires less finesse.			

Music for School and Amateur Orchestras (*cont'd.*)

Title	*Publisher*	*Grade*	*Score*
Pergolesi: *Concertino in B-flat* Somewhat complicated (Four violins).	Ricordi	4-5	Full
A. Scarlatti: *Concerto in E Major* Easy, except for E Major key.	Ricordi	4-5	Full
Handel-Harty: *Polonaise, Arietta, Passacaglia* Modern orchestration, sounds well.	Boosey	4-5	Full
Grieg: *Lyric Pieces* Mostly strings.	Peters	4-5	Full
Bach-Stokowski: *Siciliana* Strings.	Broude	4-5	Full
English Instrumental Music of 16th and 17th Centuries (2 vols.) Mostly strings. Composers Bull, Byrd, etc. Consort music.	Peters	3-6	Full
Guion: *Arkansas Traveler* American folk tunes, arranged.	Schirmer	3-6	Piano
Flotow: Overture to *Martha* The old "war horse" is still effective.	Boosey	3-6	Full
Guion: Two Pieces from "*Texas Suite*"	Schirmer	3-6	
Flotow: Overture to *Stradella*	Fischer	3-6	Full
Liadov: *Musical Snuff Box* Charming when done with precision.	Schirmer	4-5	Piano
Mahler: *Adagietto* from *Fifth Symphony* Strings and harp (piano) not hard but highly sensitive.	Peters	4-5	Full
Purcell-Wood: *Trumpet Voluntary* Good trumpets needed.	Chappell	3-6	Full
Offenbach (Dorati): *La Vie Parisienne* Pieces from *Gaités Parisiennes* ballet.	Mills	3-6	Piano
Offenbach (Isaac): *Ballet Parisienne* Similar to above.	Fischer	3-6	Piano
Adam: Overture to *Si J'étais Roi* Sprightly French piece.	Boosey	4-6	Full
Gordon Jacob: *The Barber of Seville Goes to the Devil* Contemporary parody, amusing.	Oxford	5	Piano
Fauré: *Pavane* Sensitive; chorus ad lib.	Broude	5	Full
Délibes: Excerpts from *Coppélia* The popular ballet.	Schirmer	4-6	Piano

Composer: Title	Publisher	Grade	Score
Brahms-Leinsdorf: Two Choral Preludes	Broude	4-6	Full
Gretry: *Tambourin*	Fox	4-6	Full
Sprightly eighteenth-century arranged for full orchestra.			
Copland: *Waltz* from *Billy The Kid* ballet	Boosey	4-6	Full
Cimarosa: Overture to *The Secret Marriage*	Boosey	4-6	Full
Like Mozart, not so subtle.			
Tchaikovsky: *Sleeping Beauty Waltz*	Fischer	4-6	Piano
The popular piece.			
Benjamin: *Jamaican Rhumba*	Boosey	4-6	Full
Popular, but in fine setting.			
Lecuona: *Andalucia Suite*	Marks	4-6	Piano
Includes famous *Malaguena.*			
Gould: *Yankee Doodle*	Mills	5	Piano
Dittersdorf: *Symphony in F.*	Schirmer	4-6	Full
Grainer: *Mock Morris*	Schirmer	4-6	Piano
Grainer: *Shepherd's Hey*	Schirmer	4-6	Piano
Delius: *On Hearing the First Cuckoo in Spring*	Boosey	4-6	Full
Impressionistic.			
Delius: *Summer Night on the River*	Boosey	4-6	Full
Impressionistic.			
Rachmaninov: *Prelude in G Minor*	Schirmer	5	Piano
Copland: *Four Dance Episodes from Rodeo*	Boosey	4-7	Full
Buckaroo Holiday perhaps too difficult; Nos. 2 & 3 easier.			
Smetana: *Farmyard Frolic*	Boosey	5-6	Piano
Nice polka.			
Rachmaninov: *Polka*	Boosey	5-6	Piano
Rachmaninov: *Prelude in C-sharp Minor*	Boosey	5-6	Piano
It is *the* well-known one.			
Vaughan Williams: *Fantasia on Greensleeves*	Oxford	5-6	Piano
Flute, strings, harp (or piano); very fine.			
Thompson: *Acadian Songs & Dances*	Schirmer	4-7	Full
Typical of this American composer's work.			
Moussorgsky: *A Night on Bald Mountain*	Fischer	5-7	Full
Muczynski: *Dovetail Overture*	Schirmer	5-7	Full
A gay work by a contemporary American composer.			
Grainger: *Molly on the Shore*	Schirmer	5-7	Piano
"Elastic" orchestration.			

Music for School and Amateur Orchestras (*cont'd.*)

Title	*Publisher*	*Grade*	*Score*
Prokofieff: *Summer Day* (childrens' pieces)	AMP Leeds	5-7	Full
Not easy for children to play.			
Prokofieff: *Classical Symphony*	Marks	5-7	Full
Hampton Series.			
Strauss: *Rosenkavalier Waltzes*	Boosey	5-7	Full
Simplified.			
Prokofieff: *March* and *Scherzo* from *The Love for Three Oranges*	Boosey	5-7	Full
Bloch: *Suite Modale for Flute and Strings*	Broude	5-7	Full
Fine flutist needed.			
Grofé *Mississippi Suite*	Robbins	5-7	Full
Grofé: *On the Trail,* from *Grand Canyon Suite*	Robbins	5-7	Full
Rimsky-Korsakov: *Hymn to the Sun,* from *Le Coq d'Or*	Boosey	6	Piano
Wilder: *Carl Sandburg Suite*	AMP	5-7	Full
Contemporary, slightly folkloristic.			
Smetana: *Furiant* from *The Bartered Bride*	Fox	6	Full
Lively Czech dance.			
Smetana: *Three Dances* from *The Bartered Bride*	Schirmer	5-7	Piano
Kodaly: *Intermezzo,* from *Hary Janos*	Boosey	6	Full
Some interesting ceasuras.			
Hovhaness: *Psalm and Fugue*	Peters	6	Full
For strings.			
Sibelius: *Finlandia*	AMP	5-7	Full
Good brass needed.			
Dvořák: *Slavonic Dances*	Fischer, Boosey	6-7	Full
Some too difficult in concert tempo.			
Stravinsky: *Suite,* Nos. 1 & 2	AMP	6-7	Full
Large orchestration but not excessive.			
Tchaikovsky: *Trepak,* from *Nutcracker Suite*	Presser	6-7	Full
Ditson Concert Series.			

Griffes: *Poem for Flute and Orchestra*	Schirmer	6-7	Full
Among finest American impressionistic works; two horns, percussion, harp, strings.			
Weinberger: *Polka* and *Fugue*, from *Schwanda*	AMP	6-7	Full
Large orchestra, rather involved.			
Schuman: *New England Triptych*	Presser	6-7	Full
Contemporary version of American folklore (rental).			
Schuman: *Credendum*	Presser	6-7	
(Rental).			
Schuman: *Newsreel*	Schirmer	7	Full
Witty.			
Gershwin: *Rhapsody in Blue*	Music Publishers Holding Corp.	6-7	Full
A first-rate pianist is needed.			

The Standard Repertory*

In addition to the information in the foregoing table, the conductor will want to know which masterworks to choose from the standard repertory.

BAROQUE

The concerti grossi of Scarlatti, Corelli, Sammartini, Vivaldi, Geminiani, Manfredini, Locatelli, and especially Handel are within the proficiency of a student orchestra. They provide a solid foundation for string players. This applies also to other baroque works, by Lully, Krieger, Purcell, Rameau, and Telemann. (Broude, AMP, Peters, Oxford, Schirmer, Carl Fischer, and Boosey have arranged or edited versions of such works.)

Bach's *Brandenburg Concertos* require accomplished solo work. If there are available a capable violinist, flutist, and pianist, the Fifth is recommended. The Fourth, with two solo flutes (orig-

* This section may repeat some observations made in Chapter 22; it is more specific, however, about the difficulties of the different works.

inally recorders) and a solo violin, is one of Bach's most charming compositions. A good solo flutist is needed for his Suite No. 2. This piece is especially suitable for young string players because of its diversity. (AMP).

Carl Philipp Emanuel and Johann Christian Bach, Johann Stamitz, Boccherini, Dittersdorf, and Boyce wrote a number of early classical symphonies within the scope of non-professionals. These works do not require the delicacy needed to play Mozart (Peters, AMP, Schirmer).

HAYDN

Many of Haydn's symphonies are excellent material for young orchestras and especially recommendable for training purposes. Among the early ones No. 12 (Peters) is worth while (the key of E major may cause some difficulties). The *Lamentatione* (No. 26; AMP) is one of Haydn's first "romantic" works, and as such especially interesting. Another "romantic" symphony is No. 44, the "tragic" (*Trauer;* AMP, Peters). The famous *Farewell,* No. 45 (Peters, AMP, Boosey), is dramatic, too, and toward the end, nostalgic. (Concerning the second movement see page 153.) The minuet and the final adagio are in F-sharp major, a difficult key. This and the following symphony (Peters) are amazingly sensitive works. Were it not for the B major key, No. 46 would technically be one of Haydn's easiest symphonies; since it is such a fine work, a transposition to C major would make excellent study material for young orchestras. (Such tampering with a masterwork seems permissible when one realizes that concert pitch in Haydn's time was at least a half tone lower than it is today. B-flat major would be more correct, but not so easy.) *La Passione* (No. 49; Peters) is another interesting work, as the title implies. Among Haydn's later symphonies, No. 82 (*L'Ours, the Bear*; Kalmus) is simple but rewarding. An especially delightful work is the well-known No. 88 (AMP), which is not easy but is within the scope of better non-professional orchestras.

Haydn's twelve *London* symphonies are all masterworks, requiring subtlety and maturity from the players. Accomplished student and amateur orchestras should be able to perform them, depending upon the competence of the different sections of the ensemble. The young conductor should study them all, then decide which to select. Recommended is No. 95 in C Minor: it has been unduly neglected (it forecasts Beethoven) and is not so difficult as some of the others. A good solo cellist is needed for the trio of the minuet.

MOZART

The mature masterworks, though technically not beyond the competence of a young orchestra, require extreme delicacy and sensitivity from both conductor and players. In Mozart's case only a few of the early (and easy) symphonies can match the later works. One of the first of his more dramatic symphonies is No. 25 in G Minor (K. 183; AMP, Broude). Two that have special charm are No. 29 in A Major (K. 201; Peters, AMP, Broude), and No. 33 in B-flat Major (K. 319; Broude, AMP). The famous No. 40 in G Minor (K. 550) is often performed by amateurs, but they cannot do justice to this great work, in which every note on every instrument must be perfect.

Two of Mozart's overtures are suited for non-professionals, the *Seraglio* (Broude, AMP) and *Titus* (AMP).

Many selections from the ballet music, *Les Petits Riens*, are very enjoyable. In addition, his German dances and minuets, as well as marches, are within the ability of non-professionals. While Mozart's early symphonies lack the depth and refinement of his later ones, other works in similar form are delightful. In his serenades and divertimentos he did not try to be "symphonic"; they abound in youthful exuberance and lightheartedness. The Serenade in D, K. 204 (AMP) is recommended, but a good solo violin is needed. The Serenade in D, K. 239 (AMP), requires a competent string quartet, but the accompanying string orchestra and timpani are easy. Among the divertimentos there is the amazing K. 131 in D (AMP) which Mozart composed at the age of sixteen. (Some movements require four horns.) The K. 287 in B-flat (AMP), is a fine work, slightly more difficult; as is K. 334, in D (AMP, Broude), with the well-known minuet.

BEETHOVEN

Greater technical skill is required by Beethoven than his predecessors demanded. His music is in the grand style, however; it captivates by its force and dramatic effectiveness, and for that reason performances of his work do not need the delicacy of Mozart. If the conductor himself has absorbed the music he should be able to tackle some of Beethoven's symphonies with non-professionals. (They love playing Beethoven and will make a special effort to overcome technical difficulties.) The First Symphony makes a good beginning. It offers few problems and although it is his first, it is clearly Beethoven. The Second Symphony is slightly more complicated, but within the scope of students. The Fifth is so frequently performed by great orchestras that a conductor may hesitate to play it with less accomplished musicians. The difficulties can be overcome, however, because the work is extremely dramatic and, among the great symphonies, the one best suited for a non-professional group. The *Eroica* is much more involved. The Seventh can be very instructive because of its persistent rhythms, but the constant pattern in the first movement may prove to be too much of an obstacle (see page 131). The less dramatic Fourth, the *Pastoral*, and the Eighth require, because of their greater delicacy, a more refined approach; none of them is easier than the dramatic ones. (All are available in many editions.)

Among Beethoven's overtures the *Egmont* (Boosey) is recommended. His three *Leonore* overtures all have similar technical problems. The Third is most suitable because of its great dramatic impact (Boosey). The *Coriolanus* overture is an excellent piece for a study of rhythm (Boosey, AMP). A performance should be attempted, however, only if the rhythmic pattern can be executed with enough clarity. (See p. 62.)

An early and not very significant work by Beethoven especially suited for beginners is the *Ritter* (Knight's) ballet (Kalmus). His more important *Prometheus* ballet (Kalmus) has dramatic and graceful sections within the ability of non-professionals. (Beethoven used the theme of its finale for the last movement of the *Eroica.*)

SCHUBERT

Probably no work in the entire symphonic literature is performed as often, by any kind of orchestra, as Schubert's *Unfinished* Symphony (many editions). Technically it is not difficult; it is in fact easier than most of Mozart and Beethoven. It is an expression of early Viennese romanticism, however, and as such requires the finest shadings and blendings (see *Workbook* for detailed analysis). Among Schubert's other symphonies, worthy of consideration are his Second (Broude, AMP), a sprightly work; his Fourth (AMP) called the *Tragic,* though this title is not quite fitting; and his idyllic Fifth. None of these works has the impact of the *Unfinished;* they do not captivate the listener as completely unless played very well. All of Schubert's *Rosamunde* music is enchanting – and certainly within the competence of non-professionals (AMP).

SCHUMANN

A professional orchestra is necessary for a good performance of any Schumann symphony. They are highly imaginative works but their orchestration shows the composer's lack of experience in this field. Schumann's overture to his opera *Genoveva,* however, deserves greater attention by any performing group. It is not easy but it is well written and if well rehearsed may be within the range of amateurs.

MENDELSSOHN

On the other extreme, Mendelssohn's orchestrations are quite brilliant. His effects depend upon clean and nimble performance.

The *Fingal's Cave* (Hebrides) overture (AMP, Boosey) might be tried by an efficient non-professional group, but it demands technical skill from most of the instruments. His *Ruy Blas* overture is effective; it is also, because of the many fermatas and tempo changes, a good study piece for young conductors. Another charming and unduly neglected work is his *Melusine* overture (Boosey). But Mendelssohn's music, it must be remembered, is never easy for an orchestra. The *A Midsummer Night's Dream* overture should not be attempted except by professionals.

THE CONCERTO

The burden on the orchestra is somewhat alleviated in the concerto, since the soloist must carry the main musical responsibility (see page 199). In any concerto, consequently, the soloist, even if he is a student, should have professional standards.

To begin with Bach, the Piano Concerto in D Minor is a great work and very instructive for the strings, as is the Concerto in D Minor for Two Violins. A neglected though very fine work is his Triple Concerto in A Minor, which has the same instrumentation as his *Brandenburg* Concerto No. 5.

Haydn wrote many concertos, non-problematic, for violin piano, horn, and trumpet, as well as the celebrated Cello Concerto in D Major (which is not available in the original orchestration). Boccherini's Cello Concerto is also a fine piece. Mozart wrote many notable concertos for piano, violin, flute, oboe, bassoon, and horn, many within the capacity of young orchestras. Beethoven's First, Second, and Third Piano Concertos are suitable for non-professional groups; but his Fourth and Fifth require greater proficiency and sensitivity, as does his Violin Concerto.

Two fine romantic works are Weber's *Konzertstück* and Mendelssohn's Piano Concerto in G Minor (both Broude). The last movement of Schumann's Piano Concerto in A Minor may create, for amateurs, unsurmountable problems in rhythm; however Schumann composed the first movement independently as a *Fantasia* and added the two other movements four years later:

therefore it is permissible to play it alone (Broude, Peters, AMP).

Chopin, who was not really an orchestral composer, limited the accompaniments of his two concertos (in E minor, Broude; in F minor, AMP) to secondary roles. The orchestral parts may not be very interesting but, with a competent pianist, these works will serve as good starting concertos for young orchestras. Liszt's two concertos – the First in E-flat (Broude) and the Second in A (Kalmus) – need a virtuoso pianist and a very accomplished orchestra. The composer was a great master of orchestration and these works have scintillating colors. The orchestra itself can sound like a virtuoso instrument; if a good conductor masters the scores, he may be able to lead even a non-professional group over all the hurdles.

Recommended among later works are Franck's *Symphonic Variations* for piano and orchestra (Kalmus) and Bruch's Violin Concerto in G Minor (Broude), as well as the very popular Piano Concerto in A Minor by Grieg (Broude). Lalo's slightly "tricky" *Symphonie Espagnole* may be appropriate (Broude, AMP), as are the many concertos by Saint-Saëns (piano, violin, cello). A fine and worthy American work is MacDowell's Second Piano Concerto in D Minor (AMP).

LATER ROMANTICS

In the symphonic literature of the nineteenth century a popular but not easy work is Franck's Symphony in D Minor (Boosey). The symphonies of Brahms, Bruckner, and especially Mahler are best left to professional orchestras, although in the case of Brahms the interpretive difficulties outweigh the technical ones. Brahms's *Academic Festival Overture* is an engaging and effective work and within the grasp of non-professionals, as are his famous Hungarian dances (Nos. 1, 3, 5, 6 in many editions). His *Serenade in D*, one of his first orchestral works, should also be considered.

In the later nineteenth century, the orchestra developed in size and technical demands but, in spite of this, the music is more accessible for non-professionals. In the music of Mozart every note must be absolutely right. In later romantic music as well, of course, *wrong* notes are not permissible; still, when a player submerges in a large mass of tone, he can — so to speak — float in the wide ocean of sound and let his emotions carry him along. The subtlety needed for classical music is thus superseded by grandeur, sensuality, and excitement.

SLAVIC MUSIC

The fact that Slavic music is most colorful and often based on folklore is one reason why it requires less interpretive refinement than classical music. There is Smetana, the Czech composer, whose *Moldau* has become one of the most popular symphonic poems and Dvořák, whose symphony, *From the New World,* was inspired by American folklore. The latter has become a great favorite, and rightly, since the music has freshness and power. Though parts of it are difficult, non-professionals can give quite acceptable performances of this work. Other outstanding works by Dvořák are his Second and Fourth Symphonies (not quite so effective as the *New World*), his tuneful *In Nature* and *Carnival* overtures, and his rhythmically stirring Slavonic dances. His Cello Concerto is one of the best, but rather difficult for the orchestra.

Tchaikovsky's music has always been very popular, particularly the last three symphonies. The Fourth and Fifth seem more difficult than they actually are; a good non-professional orchestra should find rehearsing and performing either a rewarding experience.

Like the Tchaikovsky symphonies, Rimsky-Korsakov's *Scheherazade, Capriccio Espagnol,* and *Russian Easter* overture are less difficult to play than they sound. They do require competent players for particular instruments (solo violin, clarinet, flute). The conductor must know his group before deciding which to choose.

Another fine Russian work is Borodin's Second Symphony,

which is technically less intricate than most of the music of Rimsky-Korsakov or Tchaikovsky.

THE STAGE

Some works originally written for the stage have become favorites in the concert hall, such as Grieg's *Peer Gynt* suite and Bizet's *L'Arlésienne.* The most popular music in the latter's *Carmen* is available in suite form. All these pieces offer possibilities for a good non-professional orchestra.

Many overtures and excerpts from Wagner's operas have been transferred to the concert hall. Wagner was a wizard of orchestration; his works appear to be quite difficult but a number of them are playable by fairly advanced groups. The prelude to *Die Meistersinger* is recommended. Somewhat easier is an arrangement from this opera comprising the dance of the apprentices and the entrance of the Meistersinger; it is not a "medley," because it follows the sequence of the opera closely. The introduction to Act Three of *Lohengrin* (with the bridal chorus) is another popular piece, and with enough good violins even the prelude to Lohengrin is feasible. The procession to the cathedral from this opera is within the range of a student group. The larger part is for wind instruments only. The Good Friday music and the slightly more complicated procession to the temple of the Holy Grail from *Parsifal*, are further possible selections. The well-known *Tannhäuser* march is available in C major instead of the proper B major, a transposition that does harm to the orchestral color of the work. Besides, when played in the right tempo even in C, it is not at all easy for strings. The B major original is difficult.

TWENTIETH CENTURY

A few shorter contemporary pieces, not too demanding, have been listed in the table. After Wagner, however, Richard Strauss carried orchestration to a new peak. He generally demands the utmost even from professional musicians, and, in fact, most contemporary composers have been writing with the idea of being performed only by orchestras with virtuoso standards. One of the few exceptions to the rule is Paul Hindemith, as the table makes clear. Copland's *Outdoor* overture is an example of music written especially for a school group, although the orchestra will have trouble in some places with the intricate rhythm (syncopation). What is really needed is more music by present-day composers written for orchestras with less than virtuoso technique.

SHOW MUSIC

One indigenous American branch of music, which has become popular all over the world, is the music for Broadway shows. Since the enormous success of *Oklahoma* American musicals have taken the place of the Viennese operetta – which had such a protracted existence during the nineteenth and early part of the twentieth centuries. Composers of show music do not pretend to the profundity of masters but a large part of their output is good music indeed.

Schools and colleges sometimes perform these musicals, and conductors looking for orchestral works will find that every good show has had its music published as an orchestral medley. Most have been compiled and orchestrated by Robert Russell Bennett, who also orchestrated most of the shows themselves. Bennett, one of the masters in the field, knows how to make an orchestra sound full and skillful without asking for overly involved orchestral technique. The orchestrations are for ordinary symphony orchestra (usually only one oboe and bassoon, but three trumpets). Ad libitum saxophone parts are also available. The young conductor should not hesitate to put one of these medleys on his program. His players will enjoy performing them and his audience will enjoy listening. Because of the medley character, which involves a great deal of gradual as well as sudden tempo (and meter) changes, this music offers many interesting conducting problems. In the Bennett arrangements transitions from one song to another are all done in good musical taste: in fact, musicianship on the part of the conductor is needed to avoid spoiling their subtlety.

The following shows are published in Bennett arrangements: *Oklahoma; South Pacific; The King and I; Porgy and Bess; Can-Can; My Fair Lady; Camelot; The Sound of Music; No Strings; Finian's Rainbow; Flower Drum Song.*

Glossary of Instruments

English	*Italian*	*German*	*French*
piccolo	flauto piccolo (ottavino)	kleine Flöte	petite flûte
flute	flauto (traverso)	(Quer-) Flöte	flûte traversière
hautboy, oboe	oboe	Oboe (Hoboe)	hautbois
English horn	corno inglese (formerly oboe da caccia)	englisches Horn	cor anglais
clarinet in B-flat	clarinetto in Si bemolle	Klarinette in B	clarinette en si bémol
clarinet in E-flat	clarinetto piccolo	Es Klarinette	clarinette en mi bémol
bass clarinet	clarinetto basso (clarone)	Bass-Klarinette	clarinette basse
bassoon	fagotto	Fagott	basson
double bassoon, contra bassoon	contrafagotto	Kontrafagott	contrebasson
(French) horn	corno (da caccia)	(Wald-) Horn	cor (de chasse)
trumpet in A	tromba (clarino) in La	Trompete in A	trompête en la
cornet	cornetto	Kornett	cornet-à-pistons
trombone	trombone	Posaune	trombone
tuba	tuba	Tuba	tuba
kettle drums, timpani	timpani	Pauken	timbales
bass drum	gran cassa	grosse Trommel	grosse caisse
side drum, snare drum	tamburo militare	kleine Trommel	tambour militaire
cymbals	piatti	Becken	cymbales
harp	arpa	Harfe	harpe
piano (forte)	pianoforte	(Hammer-) Klavier	piano
organ	organo	Orgel	orgue
violin	violino	Violine (Geige)	violon

Glossary of Instruments (*cont'd.*)

English	*Italian*	*German*	*French*
viola (in England, tenor)	viola (da braccio)	Viola (Bratsche)	alto
violoncello, cello	violoncello	(Violon-) Cello	violoncelle
double-bass contra-bass, string bass	contrabasso (violone)	Kontrabass	contrebasse

Index

Index

*Index of Musical Examples and Analyses**

* Page numbers in italic.

Index of Musical Examples and Analyses